Bikes

Bikes

Thirty Years and More of the Motor-Cycle
World Championships

by

Mike Hailwood
with Peter Carrick

Technical Review by Vic Willoughby

NEW ENGLISH LIBRARY

The pictures in this book are reproduced by courtesy
of *Syndication International* and *All-Sport
Photographic*.

First published in Great Britain by New English Library,
Mill Road, Dunton Green, Sevenoaks, Kent, a division of
Hodder and Stoughton Ltd, in 1982

Printed in Great Britain by St Edmundsbury Press,
Bury St Edmunds, Suffolk
Bound by Dorstel Press, Harlow, Essex
Typeset by Rowland Phototypesetting Ltd, Bury St Edmunds, Suffolk

British Library Cataloguing in Publication Data
Hailwood, Mike
    Bikes.
    1. Motorcycle racing—History
    2. Motorcycle World Championships—History
    I. Title   II. Carrick, Patrick
    796.7'5   GV1060

ISBN 0 450 04878 0

Contents

Acknowledgements

Numerous people and organisations have helped with
BIKES. Thanks are extended to them all, in particular Vic
Willoughby, Mick Woollett, Pauline Hailwood, the Auto-
Cycle Union, *Motor Cycle Weekly*, *Motor Cycle News*, and
Beverley Mortimer, who typed the manuscript.

Illustrations 1–9 inclusive, and 15 (top) are reproduced by
permission of Syndication International; 10 (top) by permission of Tony Duffy; the remainder by permission of All Sport.

Foreword

by Pauline Hailwood

AFTER MIKE died there was no commitment on Peter Carrick's part to show me what he and Mike had written in *Bikes*. I am grateful that he did and I am glad to see the book published.

Although Mike left motor-cycle racing for cars, bikes were always his first love and his successful come-back rides on the Isle of Man gave him great joy and satisfaction. It is right and just, therefore, that his final commentary should be on motor-cycle racing and, indeed, on the World Championships where he achieved so much success and international recognition.

Mike was a great lover of life and looked forward rather than back. In *Bikes* the reader is able to share in the world which meant so much to him for so many years – a world which responded with its respect and admiration.

It is my wish that *Bikes*, Mike's final book, will be an unqualified success. I know that is what he would have wanted.

Pauline Hailwood
1982

Introduction

I FIRST met Mike Hailwood in London's Hilton Hotel in Park Lane in the 1960s when he was at the peak of his motor-cycling career. I wanted to work with him on his autobiography but, disappointingly for me, he had the book already planned with his friend and colleague, Ted Macauley.

The last contact I had with him was in October 1980 when he (in a studio in Birmingham) and I (in a studio in London) took part in a phone-in radio programme on London Broadcasting to mark the publication of my *Guinness Guide to Motor-Cycling*. By that time he had decided to do this book with me on the World Championships. We had completed our early discussions and agreed what he wanted to include. The final couple of interviews were about to be arranged when he and his young daughter Michelle were so tragically killed in a car crash in March 1981.

Mike Hailwood was a brilliant and successful motor-cycle racer. He lived down his privileged background and a doting millionaire father, and in the tough, uncompromising world of motor-cycle racing, gained universal respect and admiration to become the most popular bike man Britain has ever produced.

It was always my ambition as a writer to work with him on a book such as this. I was delighted when, after a few discussions and some slight hesitancy over terms – for Mike was never a pushover in a business deal – he happily agreed and the contract was signed.

Now the book is a reality. It is Mike's last book, published posthumously. It is my wish, and that of his colleague over many years, Vic Willoughby, who wrote Chapter 4, that he would have been well satisfied with the result. *Bikes* is dedicated unreservedly to his memory.

PETER CARRICK

ONE

1949 . . . and the First World Champions

Motor-cycle racing didn't hold much interest for Mike Hailwood in 1949. The road-racing fans showed even less interest in Mike Hailwood, even though by then, as a somewhat undisciplined nine-year-old, he used to bustle around the sumptuous lawns of the Hailwood mansion in Oxford on his mini-motor bike. They had much more important things to get excited about – like a brand-new series of world championships which started that year. Twelve years later I was to win that world championship for the first time, and for almost a decade the world-championship series was to be the basis of my racing career.

But in 1949 it wasn't Mike Hailwood, but a daring and talented rider called Les Graham who was the British racing hero as he hurtled his AJS Porcupine machine round the grand-prix circuits of Europe to become the first-ever 500 cc World Champion. Those were adventurous, optimistic days. The war had been won, British motor cycles were still clinging grimly to their pre-war reputation for being the best and most reliable in the world, and the country's crusading spirit had not yet surrendered to the unbounded post-war energy and ingenuity of the Japanese and the Germans. Les Graham fitted into the pattern ideally. He had served in the war as a bomber pilot in the RAF, had been honoured with the Distinguished Flying Cross, and as motor-cycle racing climbed to its feet again after six years' enforced absence, he was well placed to build on his pre-war reputation gained mainly on British circuits in the late 1930s.

By the standards of the 1980s that first world-championship series was unsophisticated, somewhat impoverished, basic and curtailed. It was ambitious to the extent that there were five machine classes (125 cc, 250 cc, 350 cc, 500 cc, and

1

sidecars), but it could hardly be called a season-long series in terms of the present world championships. Then, as now, the 500 cc class was the premier event, but only six events made up the championship programme in 1949. There were five races in the 350 cc class, four in the 250 cc class, and only three for the 125 cc and the sidecar riders.

The Isle of Man Mountain circuit was even then regarded as the premier test for both man and machine and was a stirring curtain-raiser for the 500 cc, 350 cc and 250 cc machines. Les Graham's pre-war record on the Island had been disappointing and unfortunate, his best placing being twelfth in the Lightweight TT of 1938 on an OK Supreme, and it was a dear ambition of his to win the Senior TT. In 1949 he looked set to achieve that goal as he raced the admittedly temperamental Porcupine into what looked to be a secure lead, before a failed magneto ended his hopes and he had to push the bike home.

But in Switzerland, in the second round, he was first to take the flag, beating the challenging Arcisco Artesiani on an Italian Gilera machine and Britain's Harold Daniel on a Norton. A second place in the next round at Assen in Holland, behind the Gilera of Nello Pagani, made Les Graham the leading contender for the title at this point, and although he didn't appear in the placings at the Spa circuit in Belgium in the fourth round, being forced to retire with a split tank, he made certain of the world title with victory in the Ulster Grand Prix. Pagani, however, pressed him hard, and after winning the final round of the series in Italy at the famous Monza circuit – where Graham was forced to retire after Italian rider Carlo Bandirola's crashed Gilera bounced into the AJS (bringing Graham down too) while they were furiously disputing the lead – finished only a single point behind the British rider.

In the 350 cc class Britain more than upheld her international prestige through an impressively dashing performance by the stylish Freddie Frith, a distinguished pre-war racer. He won all five rounds with new speed records in each race to give the British Velocette factory their first world championship. It was a devastating performance after which Frith, who had been racing for some nineteen years, settled for retirement.

In the other solo classes there was nothing to touch the Italian riders on their Italian machines. Pagani, on a Mondial, took the 125 cc title by winning two of the three events, and Bruno Ruffo led the famous Moto Guzzi factory to victory in the 250 cc class, though he won only once (in Switzerland). By winning two of the three sidecar events, Britain's Eric Oliver, with passenger Denis Jenkinson this year, was the first Sidecar World Champion.

It was certainly a bit extravagant to claim the new competition as a world series, since it was in every sense as European-based as the international races which had been run in various forms since the end of the war. On the other hand, the Federation Internationale Motorcycliste (FIM) should not be criticised for casting an ambitious eye to the future, though it was to be a long time indeed before any riders of significance who were other than European entered the fray for 'world' honours, and another fifteen years before the Japanese first took an interest.

But a start had been made, and altogether the series was considered to be a success and a major step forward from the events which had preceded it. These had taken various forms. Grand-prix racing in events similar to those which were to combine to form the world-championship series had really become established in the 1920s when the most traditional of the grands prix – the Italian, German, Belgian and Dutch, for instance – were first held. They took place on normal roads which in those days were roughly surfaced, and were overpoweringly long affairs, stretching the machines and riders to the limit over laps which could be fifteen to twenty miles long. The Isle of Man Tourist Trophy course, remember, was more than 37 miles round, and had been so since the adoption of the Mountain Course way back in 1911. Some races went on literally for hours and although machines were of mainly 500 cc capacity, with some 250 cc and 350 cc bikes, they often joined together in one race because the entry lists were not big enough to run separate races.

By the 1930s motor-cycle racing was better organised and a little more polished. Road surfaces were smoother, speeds higher; most European countries staged a grand prix, and public interest was stimulated by means of shorter races, which could be followed more easily and were more exciting, and by a well-organised race programme of separate classes based on the cubic capacity of the machines. British riders like Jimmy Simpson, Stanley Woods, Graham Walker, Wal Handley and Alec Bennett, swept the board on outstanding machinery which was acknowledged to be the best in the world: Rudge, AJS, Sunbeam, Velocette and, of course, Norton. In such an atmosphere the so-called Continental Circus had its origins, with riders contracted to race for certain factories, travelling direct from one race to another. Nowadays, the star riders can travel by private plane and stay in luxurious hotels, or move from one race to another in purpose-built mobile homes, lavishly appointed and often presented free of charge by the manufacturer in return for the spin-off prestige and publicity value. In the 1930s it was much more rugged. A factory's riders, mechanics, tools and machines made up the same party and travelled by train from one circuit to another.

In those pre-war years, British Norton machines monopolised the results in the prestigious 500 cc and 350 cc classes. Scotland's Jimmy Guthrie was perhaps their most outstanding rider of the period, dominating the grand-prix scene and winning at one point nine 500 cc continental races in a row. Tragically, he was killed in the German Grand Prix of 1937. As the war clouds gathered, Britain's superiority was seriously challenged by the supercharged power of the 500 cc flat-twin BMW from Germany, and in the 250 cc and 350 cc classes by that country's DKW two-stroke machinery. International prestige in sporting events of all kinds was a firm policy of Hitler's National Socialism doctrines and the investment set aside to help gain sporting honours did a lot to hoist Germany to the surface of motor-cycle sport. As the world tottered on the verge of war, the Italians also made their mark: the water-cooled, supercharged Gileras, though not always reliable, were powerful enough to beat the BMWs.

In the meantime, the individual races had been formed into a European Championship series, similar in basic structure to

4

the post-war World Championship. This idea was introduced in 1938 with little fuss by the predecessor of the FIM, the Federation Internationale des Clubs Motorcyclistes (FICM), and was continued in 1939 when, because of the outbreak of war, the nine scheduled races were reduced to seven. The Italian Gilera factory took the coveted 500 cc title through Dorino Serafini; Britain's Ted Mellors was the 350 cc title-holder on a Velocette, and Ewald Kluge, on a German DKW machine, won the 250 cc title, also becoming Champion of the Year for the second time. This particular accolade was granted to the winner with the most points from all classes.

Having thus established a series-based competition before the outbreak of war, it seemed surprising that it took until 1949 for the idea to be taken up again and launched as a 'world' series. There were a number of reasons for this: it took established riders some time to get back into racing; Germany was banned from international competition because of the war – a fate from which Italy, incidentally, totally escaped; and, perhaps most of all, because of far-reaching decisions taken by the FICM at their first post-war congress in London in December 1946.

These must have astonished even the most informed observers. For Britain, although it had most to lose by the change, advocated the use of normally available pump-grade fuel only, and Italy, though their delegation must have known that it would effectively outlaw their most important racing challenge from the Gilera factory, suggested that supercharging be banned. Both proposals were ratified and factories were left with some hard thinking to do. Britain fared better than Italy. The single-cylinder Nortons and Velocettes were adapted for the use of 72-octane fuel (before the war, a mix with pure Benzole had given them an almost 100-octane fuel to race on), and while performance suffered they could at least compete. Not so the water-cooled Gileras which had survived the war and were ready to race again. The ban on superchargers killed them off and, incidentally, put paid to an ambitious 500 cc supercharged twin which Velocette had completed in 1939 and were about to unveil in championship races.

There is one curious point about these measures taken by the FICM in 1946. Why did the British and Italian delegations put forward these proposals, knowing that they each stood to lose most by their implementation? I have tried in vain to solve that riddle. Most books and reference papers mention it, but not one that I have read gives the reasons for these surprising moves.

There were a few races in 1946 and then, in 1947, six recognised grand-prix events took place, each run independently. The year was notable for the introduction of the AJS Porcupine, which caused a sensation when seen for the first time at the first post-war TT that year. Unfortunately the Isle of Man races were more domestic than they need have been, the Italians supporting the Swiss Grand Prix, which had been organised for the same time and which, that year, was also designated the Grand Prix d'Europe. If one of the organisers had been willing to compromise, the top riders could have competed in both races, but there was no conciliation on that point and riders were left to choose which meeting to support.

The new 500 cc AJS Porcupine was the first completely new factory racer to appear in this very first post-war TT meeting on the Isle of Man, but the reliability of the single-cylinder Nortons won the day, with Harold Daniel taking the Senior event and Artie Bell finishing second.

Meanwhile, in Switzerland, a Moto Guzzi ridden by Omobono Tenni won the 500 cc event on a V-twin developed from the Italian factory's pre-war successful racer, and the Italians also secured the 250 cc and sidecar events; but Fergus Anderson on a private Velocette he had bought from the factory maintained British prestige by winning the 350 cc race.

These early post-war efforts were commendable, for it has to be remembered that factories were struggling to build up their businesses in the face of extreme difficulties in a world where many essential items were scarce and which was still economically depressed. With fuel rationed at a pitifully low level in Britain, it was a miracle that any racing took place at all.

There was no change in the structure of racing for 1948 and the same six events were once again organised as a grand-prix programme, each promoted as an individual meeting with no news of a possible championship series breaking the surface. With commendable fortitude, both the British and the Italian factories had been working hard on new racing machinery, and during the year AJS introduced their famous 350 cc 7R, and Gilera a new four-cylinder unblown model, which was first seen at the Dutch TT. Nortons ridden by Artie Bell and Harold Daniel proved superior, notwithstanding the new Gilera, which proved difficult to handle.

The year witnessed good performances by Jock West on the AJS Porcupine and by Les Graham on a similar machine. Graham showed the kind of form which was to make him the first 500 cc World Champion the very next year when he raced ahead of the Norton team in Belgium with an impressive lap at 93.75 mph; but he was forced to retire, leaving the way clear for Johnny Locket on a Norton. It was in the 350 cc race in Belgium that post-war machine development was seen to have closed the gap opened by the enforced use of low-octane fuel. For the first time on a grand-prix circuit a pre-war lap record was broken, Bob Foster rushing his Velocette round at 90.37 mph against Stanley Woods's pre-war best, also on a Velocette, of 89.94 mph.

The racing season ended with a grim Ulster Grand Prix held in pouring rain, but with the glory of being the Grand Prix of Europe that year, and an Italian Grand Prix which lost much of its impact by being switched to a small, almost unknown circuit from its traditional home at Monza, and clashing with the important International Six-Days Trial.

But later that year the FICM at their annual congress not only decided to revert to a championship series of races, but added to its status by declaring it to be the *world* championships. Thus the modern series, as we saw at the beginning, was started in 1949 and has been run in substantially the same form since then. Along the way there have been some changes, particularly governing the eligibility of machines and the methods of scoring points. In 1949 the first five riders home gained points – 10 for the winner, 8, 7, 6 and 5 for second, third, fourth and fifth places; there was a single point awarded for the rider racing the fastest lap, but only if he

7

finished the race. Unlike later, when the number of races was considerably increased, and the results from all the meetings counted towards the championships.

TWO

Britain Supreme. Then Italy and Germany Take Over

In the 1920s and 1930s British-made motor cycles had an unparalleled reputation throughout the world. Racing success had done much to put them in a class of their own, but by 1950 the great days of Norton, AJS and Velocette were virtually at an end in top-level international road racing. The 125 cc and 250 cc classes were dominated by Mondial and Guzzi from Italy, with Benelli and Morini in strong support. Poised to move in on the most prestigious 500 cc class were those fabulous multi-cylinder machines from the Gilera factory at Arcore in Northern Italy. Throughout the 1950s and until the Honda phenomenon of the early 1960s, world-championship racing would be dominated by Italy, whose machines, together with some very capable NSU racers from Germany, were to lock the door firmly on Britain's failing efforts.

Gilera were by no means unknown. They had by 1939 already established a number of important world records, that year winning the European road-racing championship with an elegant 500 cc four-cylinder machine, water-cooled and supercharged, which was a highly developed version of their historic 1934 Rondine. But for the banning of supercharging in road racing after the war, there is little doubt that Gilera would have become world champions earlier. Although their handling was less efficient, the multi-cylinder Gileras were much quicker than the single-cylinder Nortons. But in 1950, at any rate, the tide hadn't completely turned against Britain. Bob Foster, Les Graham and a new sensation called Geoffrey Duke, a member of the Norton works team for the first time, kept Britain strongly in the picture and Duke, riding the new, and soon to become famous, 'Feather-

9

bed' Norton with its superb qualities of road holding, only just failed to gain the 500 cc crown.

There is no doubt that for sheer riding ability Duke had the measure of the Italian challenge and in the opening round on the Isle of Man served notice on the Gileras by rushing to a sensational record-shattering win, with Artie Bell in second place.

The next round in Belgium was even more sensational, as Britain and Italy prepared for the first major confrontation between the two countries in the 500 cc world-championship racing. The psychological advantage was Britain's. Bob Foster had already raced to victory in a 350 cc event dominated by British entries, and both Geoff Duke and Artie Bell's practice times for the 500 cc race had been better than those registered by the Gileras.

The pack of riders clung close together in that initial surge from the line, but soon Nello Pagani and Umberto Masetti raced to the front, Duke and Bell challenging strongly. Brakes were applied heavily for the exceptionally tight La Source hairpin; then, out of the bend, accelerating and roaring away in the lead, was Bandirola. Bell moved ahead of the others to chase the Italian in a tremendous challenge. Then came Pagani, Duke, Les Graham on the AJS, and Masetti. Graham's dashing style caught the attention as he moved up sensationally from sixth to second, behind Bandirola; and with Bell in third place Britain was maintaining a strong challenge. But then as Bandirola braked, Graham's front wheel brushed the Gilera and the AJS slithered out of control. Graham was flung clear, but suffered no serious injury. Bell, travelling at about 100 mph close behind, crashed into the AJS and the momentum took him and the two machines crashing into the timing box. He suffered serious injury and although he recovered it was sadly the end of his racing career.

As leader Bandirola came in sight of the grandstand once more, it was left to Geoff Duke to take up the challenge. Pagani was third, Masetti fourth. But Duke was riding superbly, and on the third lap managed to ease his Norton into the lead, only to lose it again on the next lap. As the leading riders set a searing pace in excess of 100 mph there was little doubt that British hopes now rested with Duke. On the eighth lap he moved into the lead again and with a superb demonstration of riding, so neat and controlled, he put all of thirty seconds behind him and the chasing Italians.

He looked set to win and therefore to complete a most amazing coincidence. For Bob Foster, riding number 28, had won the 350 cc race. Britain's Eric Oliver, riding number 28, had won the sidecar event. Geoff Duke, too, was riding number 28 and also looked to be a certain winner. With less than two laps left the Englishman was still in the lead, but as he prepared to negotiate the Masta bends, he slowed down, stopped and then rode dejectedly into the pits, a major section of the tread of his rear tyre having been stripped off. Masetti went on to win, with Pagani in second place and Ted Frend, on an AJS, finishing third.

British confidence was high as the Continental Circus moved on to Holland for the Dutch TT. New tyres had been flown out from Britain, but disastrously these proved to be even worse than the originals. After only a few laps the entire Norton and AJS teams had retired. The tyre treads on Duke's machine stripped off again, this time locking the rear wheel as he braked. He crashed heavily and Umberto Masetti again rode to victory to put him well in the lead in the world-championship race. In the fourth round, in Switzerland, Dickie Dale in place of Artie Bell brought the Norton team up to strength, but it was Les Graham on the AJS who nosed ahead of the pursuing Gileras to take first place.

A switch from Dunlop to Avon tyres for Ulster improved Geoffrey Duke's confidence and on the historic Dundrod circuit he won handsomely, with Masetti and Gilera down in sixth place. Although Duke again won easily against Gilera and MV Agusta opposition in the last grand prix of the year at Monza, his ill luck earlier in the season had robbed him of his title. He had 27 points against Masetti's 28.

In some respects the Belgian Grand Prix of 1950 was a pointer to the future. There was little doubt that the Italians meant business in the 500 cc class. It was perhaps the beginning of the steady decline of Britain as a major power in

11

international road racing, despite the Italian challenge being held off courageously by Duke for another couple of seasons. It was also in Belgium that year that MV Agusta, with machines not unlike the Gilera fours with their torsion bar rear springing and shaft drive, made their debut in the 500 cc class. After the racing retirement in 1957 of all other major Italian factories, MV were to dominate the class in the longest run of successes ever recorded by one factory in world-championship racing.

The MV Agusta motor-cycle concern will always be a bit special for me because it was seven years later, in 1957, that I made my road-racing debut on a 125 cc MV racer when I was just seventeen; and, of course, I won four 500 cc championships riding the factory MV.

But back in 1950, it was the Italian Mondial factory which dominated 125 cc racing, taking first (Ruffo), second (Leoni), and third (Ubbiali) places in the world championships. Italy again triumphed in the 250 cc class, Ambrosini of Italy riding a Benelli finishing in top position, with the Moto Guzzis of Cann and Anderson, both of Great Britain, placed second and third. In solo racing, only in the 350 cc class did Britain continue to dominate the results. Bob Foster on the Velocette was world champion, Geoffrey Duke on a Norton was second, and Les Graham on the AJS was third.

Fergus Anderson, in fact, represented a trend, which was to gain momentum as the British racing effort waned, of British riders racing for foreign factories. Despite optimistic talk of Norton producing multi-cylinder machinery to compete against the Italians, nothing materialised, and top British riders with the ambition to win a world championship had increasingly to look abroad for the machinery on which they might achieve their objectives. Moreover, although in the 1950s Italy produced the faster-racing motor cycles, their riders were not in the same class as those from Britain. Fergus Anderson, shrewd and a witty journalist as well as a talented motor cyclist, had previously raced on a number of British and German machines, but living on the Continent in the early post-war years, he was handily placed to seize the opportunities that existed in riding for a continental factory.

12

Cecil Sandford and Les Graham were soon to follow suit, and by 1954 any British rider with his sights set on a road-racing motor-cycle world championship had to ride foreign machinery.

But for a while Geoffrey Duke and the Norton factory kept Britain in the picture. Duke, though not of my generation, undoubtedly had exceptional talent on a motor cycle. He combined success with a smooth, easy, fluent style which was a joy to watch. He is also remembered for bringing a new look to motor cycling. He was the first rider to wear one-piece leathers, which he invented as a means of reducing wind resistance. Against the rather shapeless two-piece suits which were then common race-wear among riders, he was an exciting trendsetter. His career, though comparatively short, lacked nothing in the way of sensation and drama. If instant success in racing is a myth, then Geoffrey Duke got close to making it a reality. He didn't leave the army until 1947, only turned with some dedication to road racing in 1949, yet was a double world champion in 1951. By 1956 his most successful years were over. At his peak, no one until then had been more universally admired, though his career at times was also turbulent. It was as much in a spirit of defiance against ill-judged comments as it was to furthering his career that he chose to ride for Gilera after 1952, and his support for a riders' strike in 1956 brought suspension by the FIM. Yet in 1951 he was undoubtedly the greatest rider in the world. He beat off significantly stronger opposition to stay on top in 1952, and for his services to motor-cycle racing he was to receive the OBE. In 1951 Duke was approaching his peak. The genius of development-engineer Joe Craig, with his new single-cylinder engine and the new McCandless frame, had given the Norton factory a stay of execution and all it required was the racing talent of Duke to keep Britain on top. Two new grands prix, in Spain and France, increased the number of 500 cc rounds to eight and when Duke didn't compete in the opening round at Barcelona and retired with ignition problems in the second round in Switzerland, British hopes looked unpromising. But three impressive wins in succession – on the Isle of Man and in Belgium and Holland – took him to the top of the points table, and a further win in Belfast placed the issue beyond doubt.

Five wins in the 350 cc class brought Duke and Norton the 350 cc title as well, Geoffrey Duke's name going down in the record books as the first rider to win two championships in one season. In the 250 cc class the talent of the Italian, Dario Ambrosini, was sadly absent. After winning the opening round in Switzerland and finishing second in the 250 cc TT, the Italian, who had battled so courageously on the lone Benelli against the superior forces of Guzzi for two seasons, was killed while practising for the French Grand Prix at Albi. Guzzi went on to take the title with ease and in the 125 cc championship there was nothing to touch the Italian Mondial factory, Ubbiali, Leoni and McCandless taking first, second and third places.

In 1952 Geoff Duke had a harder time fighting to retain his 500 cc and 350 cc world titles. If the jubilation at his remarkable success in 1951 had dimmed British eyes to the Italian threat which was so near at hand, it perhaps should not have done. A clear indication of future trends could clearly be seen at the final grand prix of 1951 when, before an ecstatic home crowd, Gilera gained a one-two-three at Monza, with Duke down in fourth place. British technology was being left well behind, though British racing motor cyclists were still the best in the world. For 1952 the Italians were cute enough to dangle some tempting carrots to persuade British riders to move on to their machines. Curiously, it was MV Agusta, less successful than Gilera at this point, who made the first successful moves to sign major British riders. Les Graham was their prime target and then, through Les, Cecil Sandford. The autocratic boss of MV Agusta, Count Domenico Agusta, with whom I was to experience contact and conflict in later years, approached Graham with a contract after the Italian Grand Prix at Monza at the end of 1950. It was an intelligent choice because Les, apart from being a superb rider, had a good deal more development experience and know-how than many of the other British riders who might have been considered as candidates. He was a dedicated rider and well respected as a person, and with fewer offers being made by British factories, who could blame him for grasping the opportunity of a major contract with a progressive factory determined to win racing honours?

It was Les Graham who gave Cecil Sandford his first MV ride. Though under contract to MV Agusta, Graham had maintained contact with Velocette and when the TT races came along he found himself faced with the prospect of riding in four races. He felt it was too many and offered Sandford one of the rides. Being of slighter build than Graham it was sensible that Sandford should take the 125 cc MV, leaving Graham to concentrate on the heavier bikes. Cecil won the 125 cc TT with comparative ease, giving the MV Agusta factory their first Isle of Man victory, and afterwards continued to ride for the factory under Graham's guidance. Later, Bill Lomas and Dickie Dale had rides for the Italian concern.

Holding out against a foreign contract longer was Geoffrey Duke who, though perhaps tempted by talk of big-money offers, continued to ride for Norton in 1952. He had little trouble in winning the 350 cc world championship, gaining the title for the second year running with four wins in succession in the first four races, to put twelve points between him and the second-placed Reg Armstrong, also on a Norton. It was much harder for him in the 500 cc class. The Gilera was considerably faster than the Norton, and MV Agusta, with Graham strongly contending, had moved up into the 500 cc class. But in the end it was a crash and subsequent injury which put Duke totally out of the running. It happened in a non-championship event at Schotten in Germany and Duke was fortunate to come away with only a broken arm, though it ended his racing for 1952. Masetti recaptured the title for Gilera, with Graham runner-up on the MV. Cecil Sandford, as the first British rider to win the world championship on a foreign machine, took the 125 cc title and, with the Velocette racing effort waning, Guzzi was the dominant factory in 250 cc racing, the Italian Lorenzetti gaining the world title for them with Fergus Anderson finishing in second place, only four points behind.

With the much-talked-of four-cylinder from Norton still

not emerging, there was little incentive for Geoffrey Duke to remain with the British factory, despite his obvious patriotism. The single-cylinder Nortons were by this time no match for the speedy Gileras and, reluctantly, Duke signed to race the Italian machines for 1953, taking Reg Armstrong with him to the Arcore factory. Norton, however, their will still strong, signed the Southern Rhodesian Ray Amm as team leader, also giving contracts to Ken Kavanagh and Jack Brett; and with Germany having been re-admitted to international racing by the FIM, it promised to be an eventful and hotly contested season.

Sensation and tragedy marked the opening 500 cc round on the Isle of Man. Geoff Duke's blistering opening lap was a record at 96.38 mph, but then on the second lap, as Les Graham flashed down Bray Hill at 130 mph, he lost control of the MV Agusta, crashed and was killed. The race went on with both Duke and Ray Amm hoisting the lap record still higher. Walter Zeller, on a fuel-injected works BMW, slid off at Signpost and had to retire, and Geoff Duke also had to call it a day with a badly damaged fuel tank, the result of too much throttle at Quarter Bridge. Ray Amm raced on to win and to complete an important 350 cc 500 cc TT double. Later that season, Duke won in Holland, France, Switzerland and Italy to take the 500 cc world championship for the second time, his first on the Gilera. Ireland's Reg Armstrong was second and Alfredo Milani was third to complete Gilera's all-conquering team. In the 350 cc class the British challenge might have been stronger if Ray Amm had not crashed while leading in the French Grand Prix and breaking a collar bone. After his Isle of Man win, he collected second-place points in the second round in Holland and was placed third in the next round in Belgium. Even so, he still finished third as Guzzi dominated, with Fergus Anderson securing the 350 cc world championship and Lorenzetti finishing in second place.

In the lighter classes the Italians were shocked by the success of the German NSU factory. This old-established concern, whose origins dated back to the 1870s, began building motorised bicycles in 1900 and in 1951 they produced a 500 cc supercharged twin which Wilhelm Herz raced to a new absolute world speed record for motor cycles of 180.29 mph, the first post-war record. It was not bettered for four years.

NSU's world-championship challenge in 1953 was with beautifully engineered single-cylinder overhead camshaft 125 cc and 250 cc twin racers which were just too swift for the Italians. With comparative ease Werner Haas brought them the 125cc and 250 cc championships, dislodging the Italian factories in these two classes for the first time since the world championships started in 1949.

In 1954 these superb machines did even better. Despite the natural skills of Carlo Ubbiali on the MV Agusta, NSU gained first and third places in the 125 cc class through Hollaus and Muller, and in the 250 cc class, with new machines fitted with six-speed gearboxes and improved engines, which could average more than 90 mph on the Mountain Course on the Isle of Man in the hands of Werner Haas, there was nothing to touch them. Even the previously all-conquering Guzzis could only offer a token challenge, and Haas won the first five rounds to win the championship with 32 points, NSU also taking second and third places through Hollaus (26 points) and Muller.

The 350 cc and 500 cc classes saw a spirited challenge from Norton in what was to be their last major year of full support for world-championship racing. Through the development skills of Joe Craig, their latest 500 cc machine had a more over-square engine (bore and stroke of 90 mm × 78.4 mm). For a single-cylinder 500 it was exceptionally powerful for grand-prix racing and of its type a truly classic machine. With this, and a completely new 350 cc design, they faced the mighty Guzzis and some potent AJS machines in the 350 cc championship, and, of course, the crushing superiority of the Gilera (with Duke riding) in the 500 cc class with a team of three riders, Amm, Brett and the Australian Gordon Laing. The 500 cc class was exceptionally hotly contested. Supporting Geoff Duke in the Gilera team were Umberto Masetti and Reg Armstrong; MV Agusta had Dickie Dale, Carlo Bandirola and Bill Lomas. With brand-new, streamlined machines, Moto Guzzi's three-man team was Kavanagh,

17

Anderson and Lorenzetti. For good measure AJS fielded Rod Coleman and Bob McIntyre. It was an exceptional array of rider talent and a vintage period for international racing, with five works teams supporting the world championships in the two most important classes. But in some respects it was a final fling. Development of racing specials far removed from models to be put on sale to the public was becoming a cripplingly expensive exercise, and as the sales of motor cycles began to ease off for the first time since the end of the war, factories began to count the cost of racing exposure at international level. At the end of the season Norton, AJS and NSU were all to announce their withdrawal from racing, robbing the sport of massive support. But in the meantime, the 1954 season had its share of excitement and incident.

In the 500 cc class there was nothing to touch Geoffrey Duke on the Gilera. After a second place on the Isle of Man, where Ray Amm took Norton to victory, Duke won in Belgium, Holland, Germany, Switzerland and Italy, to give him his fifth world title in four years. Norton did well to finish in second and third place through Amm and Kavanagh. Ray Amm finished in second place in the 350 cc class with New Zealand's Rod Coleman on the AJS taking third position. World champion in this class, for the second year running, was Fergus Anderson on the Guzzi. He retired from racing at the end of the season to run Moto Guzzi's competitions department.

While all this had been going on in the solo classes, sidecar racing was making its own history. Right from the start of the world championships in 1949 there had been nothing to approach the British entries in the sidecar class, and through Eric Oliver in 1949, 1950, 1951, and 1953, and Cyril Smith in 1952, they had overcome an insistent challenge from Gilera. The pattern at the start of the 1954 season looked to be similar, but there were two significant differences. First, the German BMW factory, which had made an impact in solo racing on the eve of the Second World War (Jock West winning the Ulster Grand Prix for them in 1937 and 1938 and then, in 1939, George Meier sensationally becoming the first foreign rider on a foreign machine to win the Senior TT on the

Isle of Man), was concentrating in the 1950s on the sidecar competition.

The outstanding low-speed torque and exceptional reliability of the BMW's transversely mounted, horizontally opposed engine made it ideal for sidecar racing, and they were set in 1954 to mount a major challenge, the German factory backing the efforts of Wilhelm Noll and passenger Fritz Cron. There were now eight sidecar rounds in the world championship, twice what there had been at the start in 1949, and Eric Oliver moved off to a predictable start by winning on the Isle of Man in the opening round. Wins in the next two rounds in Northern Ireland and Belgium put the British sidecar ace in a strong position, but in a minor meeting in West Germany he broke an arm and was unable to compete in the fourth round in Germany. He made a valiant attempt to retain his title by riding in the penultimate round in Switzerland, but he wasn't properly fit and while Noll on the BMW went on to record his second win in two rounds, Oliver had to be content with sixth place. By winning the final round in Italy, the German rider took the title with 30 points to Oliver's 26.

It was the start of a racing phenomenon and for more than twenty years BMW-powered sidecar outfits were supreme in the world championships. Not until 1977, twenty-four years after Eric Oliver's last victory, was the sidecar world championship won again for Britain – when George O'Dell showed the value of consistency by taking the title without winning one single round!

The second half of the 1950s started tragically. Ray Amm, intensely patriotic, had repeatedly turned down offers from non-British factories, but with Norton now in no position to produce four-cylinder machinery to compete with the best from Italy and Germany, he reluctantly signed for MV Agusta. In his very first outing for the Italian factory, on a new 350 cc four-cylinder machine, he crashed and was killed. The tragedy occurred at Imola on Easter Monday, 1955.

The year was also notable for a massive effort by Gilera, who sometimes entered six of their famous 500 cc fours in a race; for the riders' revolt over start money at the Dutch TT, which led to Geoffrey Duke being suspended for his support

19

of the riders; and, technically, for the new air-cooled DKW with its engine set across the frame which was to rival Moto Guzzi in the 350 cc class, and also for a new water-cooled 500 cc Guzzi, with a V-eight engine.

An unusual situation in 1955 concerned the British rider Bill Lomas. He was originally contracted to race AJS and Matchless machines under a 'revised racing policy' at the factory, but a row broke out at the opening round on the Isle of Man. Lomas had also arranged to ride for MV Agusta in the lightweight race and, having chosen to defy the British factory's instruction not to ride for the Italian factory, found himself without rides in the Senior and Junior events. Fergus Anderson, by then masterminding the Guzzi race effort, offered him 500 cc and 350 cc rides and Bill Lomas came away from the Island with remarkable results: a win for MV Agusta in the 250 cc race and a win for Guzzi in the 350 cc event. It was to be a great season for Bill. He went on to take the 350 cc world title with further wins in Germany, Belgium and Northern Ireland, and only missed topping the 250 cc table because of an infringement in the Dutch TT at Assen. He crossed the line first, ahead of his MV Agusta team mate Luigi Taveri, but because he failed to switch off his engine during a refuelling stop, he had to forfeit the points, leaving the veteran West German rider Herman Muller on the NSU to take the title with 19 points to Lomas' 13, Cecil Sandford on a Guzzi sneaking into second place with 14 points.

It was also in 1955 that the passionate determination of Count Agusta to see his MV Agusta race machines up in the results began to be rewarded. In the 125 cc class, MV Agustas ridden by Ubbiali, the Swiss rider Taveri, and Remo Venturi finished first, second and third in the championship. Lomas, as we have noted, brought MV Agusta a third place in the 250 cc class, and in the 500 cc championship Umberto Masetti took the Italian factory to third place, their best position in this class since Les Graham's second place in 1952.

Geoff Duke was once more supreme in 500 cc racing and by winning four classic rounds in succession took the 500 cc world championship for the fourth time in five years. His best racing years were now over. Disciplinary action imposed by the FIM because of his support of the riders' revolt in 1955 banned him from racing until July. By then a talented young rider called John Surtees had beaten the opposition in the Senior TT and in the 500 cc class in Holland, and he and Duke clashed for the first time in the Belgian Grand Prix. But the odds were too long for Duke after he was forced to retire in Belgium with a broken piston on the Gilera when he was ahead of Surtees, and later he crashed in the wet, also while in the lead, allowing John Hartle to win the Ulster Grand Prix on a Norton. An epic race in the final round in the Italian Grand Prix at Monza saw Duke collect his first championship points of the 1956 season. Gilera riders occupied the first four positions. But by then Surtees had won his first world title with comparative ease.

Through Carlo Ubbiali (in the 125 cc and 250 cc classes) and Surtees in the 500 cc class, MV Agusta enjoyed a remarkably successful season with three world championships out of a possible four. Bill Lomas kept the Guzzi flag flying in the 350 cc class, becoming world champion for the second time in two years. Bill, incidentally, was a true professional. History has under-rated him. His uncompromising attitude and his forthright comments didn't always go down well with the public and he lost some favour among British fans through his apparent reluctance to ride on British short circuits. He felt professional motor cyclists should be rewarded sufficiently to make it unnecessary for them to have to scamper after start money in other races every weekend. He told me I was an idiot to go on dashing about all over the place to ride when I held a works contract. 'Riding in the world classics should be enough,' he said. Strange that Bill should criticise me for that, because I know that, later on, that great short-circuit racer Derek Minter, who became such a favourite with the short-circuit crowds at Brands Hatch and elsewhere, felt equally that I had lost popularity by not racing often enough at home circuits.

By 1957 the great Italian era in world-championship racing was almost at an end, though at the start of the season there was no such indication. The close-season switch in factory contracts brought the brilliant Scottish rider, Bob McIntyre,

21

into the Gilera squad in place of Reg Armstrong who, incidentally, had also been banned for much of the previous season, along with Duke and a number of other riders, for his support of the riders' revolt in Holland. With Bob in the Gilera team were Geoffrey Duke, Libero Liberati and Alfredo Milani. John Surtees and Umberto Masetti spearheaded the MV Agusta challenge, while Bill Lomas and Dickie Dale had been joined by the Australian Keith Campbell on Guzzi machines. When a pre-season crash put Duke out of the first four classic rounds, and Bill Lomas had to retire from racing altogether after crashing twice, the second time in the third round in Holland, the 500 cc title looked wide open. Liberati had won in Germany, with McIntyre in second place, and the talented Scot had scored a major triumph on the Isle of Man. He not only beat John Surtees in the Senior TT, extended that year to eight laps from its usual seven, but made racing history by crashing through the 100 mph lap barrier. No other rider had raced over the Mountain Course at such speed. It was a fitting climax to the TTs which, in 1957, celebrated their Golden Jubilee.

This magnificent display by McIntyre, who had earlier, in the West German Grand Prix at Hockenheim, set up the fastest lap for any world-championship event of 129.55 mph (though Liberati went on to win the race) now put the Scot ahead in the race for championship honours. A win in Holland in the next round could have given him an outstanding chance of taking the title, but his engine misfired and he had to stop, John Surtees rushing ahead to win, with Liberati second. Two more grand-prix wins in Ulster and in Italy brought Liberati the 500 cc title to give the Gilera factory this prestigious crown five times in six years. Gilera were also outstanding in the 350 cc class, McIntyre and Liberati finishing second and third. The title was taken by Guzzi for the fifth year running, this time through the riding of Keith Campbell.

In the lighter classes Mondial came back sensationally in 1957. With superb, streamlined double overhead camshaft single-cylinder machines, they dominated both classes, taking the first three places in the 250 cc class through Cecil

Sandford, Tarquinio Provini, and Sammy Miller, who was later to become one of the greatest trials riders of all time. Mondial completed their rout of MV Agusta by taking the 125 cc title through the brilliant riding of the young and talented Provini. Consolation for MV Agusta were the second and third places in this class through Taveri and Ubbiali.

It was the end of an era, for at the end of the 1957 season, and without warning, Gilera, Guzzi and Mondial all announced their withdrawal from racing. It was a shattering blow, coming only three years after similar decisions had been made by Norton, AJS and NSU; and then later by DKW. Could racing survive such a desperate situation, particularly as MV Agusta for a time also contemplated pulling out of racing? Their morale was low, for after winning three of the possible four solo world titles in 1956, they had won nothing in 1957. But John Surtees had worked hard on improving the stability of the MV machines and felt that in 1958 they would have the measure of Gilera. He was never required to put his confidence to the test, but Count Domenico saw his chance of putting MV Agusta on top of the world and decided to continue racing.

A lot of fire went out of world-championship racing as MV Agusta were left virtually unchallenged to dominate the classics, and for the next three years they won all four solo classes in an unprecedented run of total success. But quietly, far away on the other side of the world, ambitions were being developed and know-how acquired which would soon change the entire face of grand-prix road racing. The first obvious signs came at the TT Races in 1959, when a racing unknown from Japan, the Honda factory, tentatively contested the 125 cc class. They made little real impact, certainly on the average race fan, but in a few years all that would change . . . and how!

Meanwhile, even more quietly, one Stanley Michael Bailey Hailwood was trying to make a place for himself in the racing world. I had endured the inevitable baptism, finishing eleventh on a borrowed 125 cc MV Agusta at Oulton Park, and after a few other races had gone to South Africa during the winter to gain valuable racing experience there. I entered

23

my first world-championship events in 1958 riding a 250 cc NSU and a 350 cc Norton, and a year later, in the 125 cc race of the Ulster Grand Prix in Belfast, I won my first world-championship race riding a Ducati. I had a long way to go, but it was a start. In those days John Surtees was the ultimate star, Geoffrey Duke was virtually at the end of his glorious career, and racing talent abounded: Bob Brown, Bob McIntyre, Gary Hocking, Jim Redman at the start of his outstanding international career, John Hartle, Dave Chadwick, Tom Phillis, Remo Venturi, the extremely talented Carlo Ubbiali, Tommy Robb, Ernst Degner and, among others, Derek Minter – uncompromising, tough, with a seemingly inborn feel for riding a bike at speed and who I was soon to find more difficult to beat, perhaps, than many of the greater grand-prix names of the 1960s.

Results and racing apart, the 1950s were a highly active period in grand-prix road racing. At times factory support was exceptional; there were periods of intense and extensive machine development and it was also the age when manufacturers became almost hypnotised by the possible advantages in racing of streamlining. Most factories added all kinds of streamlining to their racers, but Norton's effort couldn't be equalled. In 1953 they produced an experimental bike which was totally unorthodox in that it was designed from the start as a highly streamlined racer. It was a revolutionary machine, very low, and designed to be ridden in a kneeling position, rather after the fashion of sidecar racers. Fuel was carried in special pannier tanks, but although Ray Amm tried it in practice, both at the Dutch TT and on the Isle of Man, it was never used in world-championship racing, though, with Eric Oliver riding, it later captured a number of world distance records at the Montlhery track near Paris.

Towards the mid-1950s both Gilera and MV Agusta made news by fitting five-speed gearboxes to their 500 cc four-cylinder racers. Moto Guzzi did likewise on their racing bikes while MV, on their 125 cc machine, and NSU, fitted six-speed gearboxes. The remarkable 500 cc eight-cylinder Guzzi was never the outright success many people expected it to be, though in 1956, ridden by Bill Lomas, it set a new lap record of 95.38 mph at the German Grand Prix. And towards the end of the decade, as MV Agusta were supreme in all classes, the efforts of the East German MZ factory, a post-war successor to DKW, should not be forgotten. Their development work brought the two-stroke machine back into racing – anticipating the future two-stroke dominance in all race classes.

With most attention and glory reserved for the more glamorous 500 cc class, the ability of the Italian rider Carlo Ubbiali tends to be overlooked. His skilful and impressive riding was a feature of the 1950s and it is certain that had he not chosen to restrict his riding to the lightweight classes he would have gained far greater recognition, for his reputation was very high among those who saw him race and those he raced against.

The first ten years of world-championship racing had not been in vain. Even if the Italian 'walk out' of 1957 had been a crippling blow, the new competition was steadily increasing its influence and prestige and would shortly benefit enormously as the Japanese began to take a hand. The FIM, condemned at times for not considering the interests of riders more and accused of operating on a too lofty and monopolistic plane, had none the less made certain beneficial changes. From 1950 until 1968, the points-scoring system was that the first six riders home scored championship points in descending order – 8, 6, 4, 3, 2, and 1 – and the point for the fastest lap was dropped. They also undoubtedly acted in the interests of both riders and spectators in 1957 in limiting the use of streamlining. The factories had taken this to such an extreme that riders found increased difficulty in handling their machines, particularly in windy conditions, and spectators hated the trend because much of the machine was hidden from view behind the fairing. From 1958 the full 'dustbin' type of streamlining was forbidden and fairings were not allowed to enclose the front wheel and the rider.

The number of world-championship rounds in the five machine classes – 125 cc, 250 cc, 350 cc, 500 cc and sidecar – had been increased from 21 in 1949 to 31 by 1959 to represent the growing impact of the new 'world' series.

The Norton Legend

For all their great tradition and staggering success, Norton were not a strong bidder for world-championship honours. Their dominant days were over before the modern series took shape. By the early 1950s, when post-war racing at an international level was really moving into top gear, their glories were largely behind them, and the British factories, Norton included, were already well along the path of inevitable, if innocent, self-destruction. Norton's failure to move with the times brought down the final curtain as Britain moved tragically into a motor-cycle wilderness from which, some thirty years later, it has still not returned.

Norton's influence on the world championships stretched over the first five years. Surely, if Geoffrey Duke had not chosen to stay with them when he could have been earning much more money with an Italian factory, their racing road block would have come about sooner. He brought them the 350 cc and 500 cc world-championship double in 1951 and this, with Eric Oliver's sidecar championship, was Norton's best period. Duke brought them their only other solo championship the following year, in the 350 cc class, but with sidecar success by Cyril Smith in 1952 and Eric Oliver in 1949, 1950 and 1953, Norton's overall record of eight world championships in five years is not without a strong element of distinction. However, let us not forget the efforts of Velocette and AJS during this period. Against Norton's three solo world championships, Velocette gained two and AJS one.

Norton, nonetheless, were the most successful British factory ever in motor-cycle racing and their record on the Isle of Man, when the TT races were still part of the world-championship round, is exceptional. Founded by James L. Norton, who built his first motor cycle in 1909 and died in 1925 when only 56, it was towards the middle 1920s that the factory's enormous contribution to racing began. Although the record books show that a Norton machine won the twin-cylinder class of the TTs in 1907, this was a privately entered machine powered by the French Peugeot engine, and the factory's first official success in the TTs was recorded in 1924, Alec Bennett winning the Senior race and George Tucker the sidecar event. It was the start of Norton's racing explosion and during the remainder of the 1920s and throughout the 1930s no factory achieved greater racing performance. On the Isle of Man; at Brooklands; during those rugged, barnstorming days when the continental grands prix were being raced over dusty, cobbled roads enlivened by such natural hazards as closed gates and straying cattle; and even in America where, in the 1940s, Norton machines shattered the US-dominated Daytona meeting, the premier British factory roared to sweeping race success. Their reputation won for Britain enormous worldwide prestige and riders who raced Nortons successfully were heroes of their time – Stanley Woods, Jimmy Guthrie, Jimmy Simpson, Freddie Frith, Harold Daniel, Geoffrey Duke, Eric Oliver, Ray Amm, John Surtees, Bob McIntyre and many others. By the time I was racing significantly in the early 1960s there was still something magical about the Norton name and my first Senior TT win in 1961, when I set up the first average for the race in excess of 100 mph, was all the sweeter because I was on a Norton.

Those incomparable Norton singles were the product of the now legendary Joe Craig, development engineer and team manager during the factory's most important years; and the racing organisation which he established set new standards and had no equal in those times. Nor should the contribution of the McCandless brothers be overlooked. Their 'featherbed' frame, which showed the way with trailing-fork rear suspension, brought extensive success in those early world-championship years after the signing of Geoff Duke.

But after the Second World War life changed in many ways. It was no longer enough for Norton to produce racers which continued to hold a strong allegiance to their road-going models, and while for years they depended for success on the reliability and superior handling of those classic and comparatively simple single-cylinder engines, the multi-cylinder onslaught from Italy finally won through in racing. While they had been able to survive the serious slump which undermined

27

the British motor-cycle industry in the 1930s, it was a different story after the war.

Diminishing fortunes led to the takeover by Associated Motor Cycles Ltd in 1952, and with Honda now searching hungrily for world markets and about to overthrow most of the traditions of motor cycling, worse was to come. Financial desperation led to a re-structuring under the Norton Villiers banner in 1966 and further consolidation within the decimated British motor-cycle industry in 1973. Racing became an early casualty as factory fortunes plunged. After 1954 there was no official works racing by the old Norton concern, and production of the successful Manx Norton was discontinued after 1962. Not until the 1970s did the Norton name reappear significantly in racing at an international level, when a Formula 750 race effort backed by the John Player tobacco company, for a brief interval, captured something of the spirit of the old days.

From my own experience, the Norton, while the factory continued its slow and painstaking development of the single-cylinder motor in order to provide a production racing machine at a reasonable cost, was crying out for a multi-cylinder unit to make it competitive in international racing. Racing history, like any other sport, is littered with 'ifs' and 'buts', though it's an interesting excursion into fantasy to sit down and consider how the course of motor-cycle racing might have altered had Norton taken up the Italian challenge.

Of the Nortons I rode I preferred the 500. Of the 350s I got on better with the AJS, which combined superb handling with speed, and I always reckoned that with the Ajay I had the edge on the best 350 cc Nortons. Anyway, I won quite a few races. Of its type, however, the 500 cc Norton was the best. What it lost out to the G50 Matchless on acceleration, it more than made up for with higher top speed; and the handling of the big Norton was impeccable. Like everyone else in Britain at the time, I lived with the dream that Norton would develop a new multi-cylinder motor (though I was never intensely patriotic in the way that Duke and Amm were), for the factory had the longest continuous association with racing of any manufacturer. It never happened, but I had the satisfaction of finishing second in the 500 cc world championship of 1961, largely as a result of good Norton rides, on the Isle of Man where I came in first, and taking second place in France, Holland, Belgium, East Germany and Belfast to the mighty MV Agusta of Gary Hocking.

The Italian Giants

The vacuum left when the main British factories pulled out of racing was filled by the illustrious multi-cylinder machines from Italy. In their day those historic bikes from Gilera, Guzzi and Mondial were a match for most opposition when ridden by the temperamental Italians. Once in the hands of the superior British riders they were virtually unassailable.

Gilera, as we have seen, were thumping hard on international racing's door in those dark days immediately before the war and, but for the ban on supercharging, would undoubtedly have dominated the post-war circuits sooner. Once the earlier water-cooled blown Gilera had been redesigned as an unblown, air-cooled machine and its suspect handling improved, it was an unqualified race winner. In the first nine years of the modern world championships, Gilera claimed six world titles, all in the most prestigious 500 cc class.

The factory's history as a motor-cycle manufacturer goes back to 1909, but it was in the 1930s and the 1950s that they made an impact on racing. In 1937 Gilera took the motor-cycle world-speed record from the German BMW factory with a fully enclosed machine, highly streamlined for the times, when Piero Taruffi reached 170.37 mph. Shortly afterwards the same rider and machine broke the world one-hour record with a distance of 121.23 miles and, early in 1939, improved it still further to 127 miles, a remarkable achievement secured while travelling up and down the autostrada between Brescia and Bergamo, almost thirty miles apart. That same year Gilera won the Senior European Road-Racing Championship.

Gilera's remarkable engineer, Pietro Remor, was responsible for the Gilera comeback after the war and gradually the performance of the engine was increased until by 1956 it was developing 70 bhp at 10,400 rpm. Other racing distinctions include Bob McIntyre's historic record-breaking perform- ance on the Isle of Man in 1957, when he crashed through the barrier for the Mountain Circuit and then did three more laps in excess of the ton to win the Jubilee Senior TT. Bob also rode the Gilera to a world record for one hour at Monza, later that same year, travelling 141.37 miles, a record which I was privileged to beat – not without difficulty – some seven years later. It was a Gilera which cracked the 100 mph lap at the old Assen circuit in Holland in 1952, where Duke, two years later, raised it still further, also on a Gilera, to 105.42 mph.

Moto Guzzi's history is shorter than that of Gilera and, where Gilera's impact was with 350 cc and 500 cc machinery, Guzzi concentrated on the lighter 250 cc and 350 cc classes, taking eight world championships from their first in 1949 to their last in 1957. Earlier, however, Guzzi had made their racing name with a 500 cc flyer which was perhaps the most successful in its class in Europe in the mid-1920s, and they had a lengthy spell of success just before the war. The great Stanley Woods rode Guzzi to a double TT victory in 1935. His lightweight victory, which included a new lap record, was the first TT to be won by a spring-framed model, and the first by a foreign machine since 1911. The very next day, riding a twin-cylinder Guzzi, Woods added a second TT triumph. In the 1950s, Guzzi racing success came from the clever develop- ment work of Giulio Carcano and the shrewd talents of rider Fergus Anderson. This famous Italian factory is still remem- bered for its active, enterprising and outstanding technical contribution to racing. A particularly ambitious experimental and development programme produced a variety of machines from the famous singles to V-eight engines, and at one time Guzzi held over 120 international records. Much of this success resulted from the testing and experimentation of streamlining in the special wind tunnel which was built at Mandello del Lario, on the eastern shores of Lake Como, where the factory workshops were situated. Later, Guzzi produced sporting versions of larger-capacity machines, these being developed by Lino Tonti, which made some impression on endurance and production racing.

Mondial's contribution to those early years of world-championship racing was more than just winning races. With superbly built double-overhead camshaft machines produced by Alfonso Drusiani, they brought a totally new meaning and prestige to 125 cc racing. In 1949, 1950 and 1951 Mondial dominated the class, before MV Agusta and NSU took control, but in 1957, with new and more powerful streamlined machines, they returned to win both the 125 cc and the 250 cc world championships. The class had been something of a joke until Mondial came along.

Particularly when I was getting started in racing I rode a wide range of machines to gain experience and, of course, was looking for a winner. The double-overhead camshaft Mondial I rode in 1959 and 1960 was the ex-works machine which had helped the great Tarquinio Provini to become world champion in 1957. It was an incredible machine – a real flyer – and on British circuits I saw everybody off. I think it was at Castle Combe that I equalled the 500 cc lap record on the 250 cc Mondial. It also showed up well in world-championship races. One way or another I won a lot of races on the Mondial, though at the time I regarded it as a standby machine for the 250 cc Ducati, which had been specially developed for me. But the Mondial was incredibly fast and handled superbly.

The bottom fell out of grand-prix racing at the end of 1957 when Gilera, Guzzi and Mondial called it a day. The Italian factories' contribution to the world championships had been vividly exciting and highly successful. Of the 36 solo championships held from 1949 to 1957 they won 24, counting a useful tally from MV Agusta. The Italian factories also gained 25 second places and 21 third places. But now it was time for someone else to take over.

31

THREE

The Honda Phenomenon

A few things happened on the Isle of Man to make 1959 a bit special: John Surtees scored a Senior/Junior TT double for the second year running; the shorter Clypse Course was used for a TT for the last time; the authorities experimented by running Formula 1 500 cc and 350 cc races; and, almost unnoticed, there arrived quietly for the first time on the Isle of Man a team of riders from the unknown Honda factory in far-off Japan.

It was the subdued beginning of motor-cycle racing's modern revolution.

I considered myself a regular Isle of Man competitor by this time, having made my debut there just a year before, entering four races and finishing third, seventh, twelfth and thirteenth. Japanese machines on the famous Island, though not without promising performances in 1959, were something of a joke. The Japanese were recognised more for cameras and watches than motor cycles; and as expert copiers rather than originators. Who could have guessed that within two years they would have chalked up two world championships in bike racing with superbly engineered machines and that I, of all people, would not only have brought them their first TT win, but one of those two world titles as well?

Like the Italian factories earlier, Honda started out by using their own national riders who didn't have the experience of world-championship racing. By 1961, however, they had not only substantially improved their racing machinery, but had realised the limitations of their own riders, signing the talented and experienced Australians Tom Phillis and Bob Brown. That lesson learned, Honda raced to enormous success and rapidly revolutionised grand-prix racing. With their single-minded resolve to dominate the world of motor cycling

32

commercially, they backed their racing effort with an investment previously unheard of in the bike world. Undisclosed
sums went into research, organisation and back-up services.
They flooded the circuits with factory 'specials' and handed
out fat contracts to the riders they decided should make up
their team. Because of Honda's blind obsession with racing
domination they paid well, and works riders, perhaps for the
first time, were able to claim the right money for risking their
necks racing. Not that Honda were a pushover. It wasn't easy
to get a Honda works ride – even in their most active years –
and like most factories they often wanted a lot without paying
enough for it. They were sometimes unreasonable, unpredictable, stubborn and ruthless. But they hoisted motor cycling
out of its 'cloth-cap' image, gave it sparkle and sophistication,
and made international, jet-set heroes of their racing stars.

They had improved 125 cc machines and an impressive new
250 racer for 1960, but made little impression on the Isle of
Man and in the selected grands prix in which they competed.
Not until later in the season did their efforts begin to reap
success. By now they had signed the Rhodesian Jim Redman,
and in Northern Ireland Tom Phillis finished second, with
Redman third; Redman secured another second place in Italy
to hoist him and Honda into fourth place in the 250 cc
world-championship table at the end of the season. In the 125
cc class Redman's fourth places in the Dutch TT and the
Italian Grand Prix were Honda's best positions in that category. The season was marred, however, by the death, after
crashing at the German Grand Prix at Solitude, of Bob
Brown.

Despite Honda's challenge, there was nothing to touch the
outstanding combination of Carlo Ubbiali and MV Agusta in
both lightweight classes.

Honda's task for 1961 looked daunting, but in the end the
Italians played into their hands. With Ubbiali on the verge of
retirement, MV Agusta decided to withdraw from the lightweight classes, being content to give support to Gary Hocking
on their heavier machinery. This opened the way for Honda.
With a mass of works machines, and having signed Luigi
Taveri from MV Agusta to join Phillis and Redman in the

factory team, they excelled in both lightweight classes on their way to 125 cc and 250 cc world championships. Towards the end of the season, particularly, Honda totally dominated 250 cc grand-prix racing and ended the year by filling the first five places in the world-championship table.

If 1959, as I mentioned, had been special, then I suppose 1961 was extra special, certainly from a personal point of view. Through their British importer Honda made machines available to private entrants and Bob McIntyre and myself were lucky enough to get those fabulous 250 cc racing Hondas on loan. The Isle of Man in 1961 was really where it all began to happen for me. I was lucky enough to win three TT races in a week, which no other rider had done, and I might have made it four, but for a gudgeon pin which had other ideas. Holding a two-minute lead in the 350 cc race, and with only thirteen miles remaining for victory on the British AJS, the gudgeon pin broke. My misfortune gave Phil Read his first TT win. But in the 125 cc race I brought Honda their first Isle of Man victory and later took the 250 cc Honda to a race win. This success, along with wins in Holland, East Germany and Sweden, was enough to give me my first world championship.

Honda could be well satisfied with the season's results. Only two years after their fairly inconspicuous debut on the Isle of Man they had dominated both the classes they had entered, taking the top five places in both the 125 cc and 250 cc TTs. Tom Phillis went on to win them the 125 cc world championship. There was no doubt that here Honda were lucky. Tom fought a season-long battle with the talented German rider Ernst Degner on the extremely fast works MZ, and with only one round left the two riders had the same number of points. But at the Swedish Grand Prix, Degner dramatically walked out on the East German MZ team, defecting to the West, and was therefore left without a machine for the final vital round in the Argentine. In an effort to take the title he managed to borrow a British EMC, a water-cooled 125 machine similar to the air-cooled MZ, but it let him down. Honda dominated the race and took the first five places. Phillis was the first rider home and by virtue of the win took the championship.

Honda widened their challenge in 1962, giving strong support to the newly instituted 50 cc class and moving up with a vengeance into 350 cc grand-prix racing. On new 50 cc Hondas Taveri and the Irish rider Tommy Robb battled against factory racers from Suzuki, who had followed Honda into championship racing. The Suzuki machinery had the edge, principally because of the technical and riding brilliance of Ernst Degner. By then resident in West Germany, Degner had been recruited by Suzuki and had spent the off-season months in Japan applying his mechanical skills to the development of the factory's 50 cc racers. The improvements he made combined with his own racing skills to bring Suzuki their first world championship.

It was a different scene in the 350 cc class, however, which Honda contested for the first time. By now I had signed a contract with MV Agusta and, after what was to turn out to be a deceptive win for me on the Isle of Man, Jim Redman raced the remarkable Honda to a runaway championship. He won four of the remaining five rounds. The last grand prix of the season in this class in Finland was won by Tommy Robb, also on a Honda. These new 350 cc Hondas were enlarged versions of the highly successful 250 cc four-cylinder racer. With Jim Redman in superb riding form, they were more than a match for the aging MV Agustas, which were simply scaled-down versions of the by-no-means-new factory 500 cc racers. (The tragedy of the season was the death of Tom Phillis on the Isle of Man on a debut outing for the new 350 cc Honda.) In the 125 cc and 250 cc classes there was nothing to compare with the Honda racing machinery. Redman completed a sensational double by taking the 250 cc title, winning six of the ten grands prix; and with another dashing performance, Luigi Taveri, with six wins running, brought Honda the 125 cc world title. Honda also scooped second, third and fourth places in the 125 cc category through Redman, Tommy Robb and Takahashi, and second place in the 250 cc class through Bob McIntyre.

Honda had certainly started something when they moved into motor-cycle racing at the beginning of the 1960s. Suzuki quickly followed suit, and within two or three years the

35

Japanese, first through Honda and then Suzuki and Yamaha, had totally changed the whole atmosphere of international racing. Later, the crippling costs of battling for world-championship honours were to lead to the withdrawal of one factory after another in the all-out form known in the early to mid-1960s; but for the time being motor-cycle racing basked in another golden era.

Honda found the going harder in 1963 as Suzuki were once again the dominant force in 50 cc racing, taking first and third places through New Zealander Hugh Anderson, and Ernst Degner. Their major rival was, rather surprisingly, the West German Kreidler factory, with Hans-Georg Anscheidt who won his first world championship. Degner was the inspiration behind a new 125 cc Suzuki which, when ridden by Hugh Anderson, was well in advance of the Hondas, and Suzuki took their second world title in 1963 without much trouble. Taveri's 38 points against Anderson's 54 was the best Honda could do.

But for the second year running, there was nothing to equal the Hondas of Jim Redman in the 250 cc and 350 cc classes, and he raced to world championships in both classes. The biggest scare to Honda in the 250 cc class came from Tarquinio Provini, riding a single-cylinder Morini. The Italian moved off to a staggering and unexpectedly brilliant start by winning the first two grands prix, in Spain and Germany. Redman brought Honda the honours on the Isle of Man and in Holland and Northern Ireland, but Provini countered strongly to win in Italy and the Argentine. Redman showed his talent in the final round in Japan and, with Provini doing no better than fourth place, Honda took the title by just a couple of points.

Honda had now won seven world titles in the short space of three years and were to go on to collect nine more before the end of the 1960s, making a colossal contribution to world-championship racing. Their record is all the more remarkable when you consider that for much of the period of their success the world championships were fiercely contested, with Yamaha and Suzuki following Honda's example and pouring vast sums of money into their quest for racing recognition.

With an amazing 137 grand-prix wins and those sixteen world championships, Honda became a racing legend in record-breaking time.

Every rider in the 1960s dreamed of a Honda contract. Factory rides brought superstar recognition, the best chances of winning the big races and more money than most riders had ever thought possible from racing. You made headlines simply by signing a Honda contract. Win a few world-championship races and a world title or two and you were an international hero. The fortunate few made history simply because they held a Honda contract. Perhaps the most notable of all was the shrewd and cunning Jim Redman, whose name is instinctively linked with the golden days of Honda racing and who won all his major honours riding for the Japanese factory. Virtually unknown before an accident to Tom Phillis gave him his first Honda rides at the Dutch TT in 1960, Jim Redman did well enough to be invited to join the Honda team the following year and between 1962 and 1965 collected six world titles, all on Honda 250 cc and 350 cc machines. After the fatal accident to Tom Phillis, Redman was made the Honda team captain and continued in control until his career ended prematurely through injury towards the end of 1966.

But it was through the Australian riders, Tom Phillis and Bob Brown, that Honda made their initial impact on the grand-prix circuits of Europe. Phillis was Honda's first team captain. His factory contract was announced in March 1960, two years after he had come to Europe, and while leading the Honda team he gained the 125 cc world title. That was in 1961. He had started racing in Australia where his succession of falls gained him the nickname 'autumn leaves'. Well-liked and easy-going, Phillis was fast but not reckless.

Phillis's early team mate in the Honda camp was Bob Brown, a quiet, casual Australian, who was also recruited by Honda in 1960. He had earlier done well riding Norton machines in 350 cc and 500 cc world-championship races in 1959, gaining a good number of second and third places in both classes. Both were to die racing. Brown was killed while practising for the German Grand Prix of 1960 while Phillis, never one to resist a challenge, crashed fatally while chasing myself and Gary Hocking on faster MV Agustas. It happened during the Junior TT of 1962, after Honda had decided to have a go at winning the event with a 250 cc machine bored out to 285 cc. The faster MV Agustas had won the race for the previous four years and originally Redman was down to ride the bored-out Honda. Phillis was such a dedicated competitor for Honda that he persuaded Redman to let him ride the bike. Despite the Honda's difficult handling, he pushed the machine to the limit and tragically, on the second lap, hit the wall at Laurel Bank and was killed.

Another rider of outstanding merit who rode Hondas for a while was the talented Scot, Bob McIntyre, a much-respected figure. Bob was perhaps the finest rider never to win a world championship. His first Honda ride came in 1960 when he took over the machine which Gilberto Milani had ridden into fifth place in the Italian Grand Prix at Monza. That led to more Honda rides the following year on a factory-loaned bike, and a contract from the Japanese factory for 1962. Second places in Spain, France and Holland were followed by a fine win in Belgium. A further second place in Germany put him in line for the 250 cc World Championship, but later that year he crashed while riding an experimental Norton at Oulton Park and was killed.

Other British riders to gain recognition on Honda machinery included John Hartle, Derek Minter, and, to a lesser degree, Stuart Graham. Hartle's chance came when Geoffrey Duke, approaching the end of his career, recommended him as an experienced rider of four-cylinder machinery to the Honda chiefs in Japan. An outstandingly courageous rider, Hartle's career was frustrated and impeded by a series of serious injuries and he had all-too-few Honda rides. He was killed while racing at Scarborough in 1968. Minter was a different kind of rider, brilliant on a motor cycle and one of the most difficult men to beat of any I have raced against. His reading of a race was impeccable and his line into and out of corners superb. Too outspoken for his own career prospects, Derek was never forgiven by Redman and the Honda hierarchy for outdoing them on the Isle of Man in 1962 when, on a loaned Honda machine more than a year old, he outrode and outwitted the official Honda team to win the 250 cc TT.

Stuart Graham's misfortune was that his works contract with Honda came as the factory was beginning to lose interest in grand-prix racing. After experience on a 350 cc AJS and a 500 cc Matchless, a privately entered Honda in 125 cc events in 1961 led to an approach from Ralph Bryans, then riding for Honda; but that wasn't until 1966, when Honda had lost the zest for championship racing. Probably his best performance was his first place in the 450 cc TT of 1967 on Suzuki.

Luigi Taveri, the diminutive Swiss rider, did well in the early days of Honda after being prominent in the 1950s with MV Agusta. He signed for Honda in 1961 and brought the Japanese factory the 125 cc world championship in 1962, 1964 and 1966; and he was second in 1963.

Ralph Bryans was one of two Irish riders to race works Hondas. The other was Tommy Robb, who signed for the Japanese factory for the 1962 season. Robb was already something of a veteran in terms of racing experience, and was brought to Honda's attention by distributor Artie Bell and Honda racing manager Reg Armstrong. After winning the 250 cc class of the Ulster Grand Prix and other good rides in Japan, he ended the season in third place in both the 125 cc and 350 cc tables in 1962, but in 1964 his contract was terminated.

Ralph Bryan's contract with Honda came later, just after he had signed to ride for the Spanish Bultaco factory. The offer from Honda team captain Jim Redman was too good to miss and Bultaco, sportingly, released him from his obligations so that he could ride for Honda. In that first season with Honda he finished second to Hugh Anderson in the 50 cc world championship, winning in Holland, Belgium, West Germany and Japan. This was a remarkable performance for a rider of only limited experience of racing in the classics. He became 50 cc World Champion riding Honda machinery in 1965, but had little further opportunity as Honda's interest waned.

My own full contractual commitment to Honda came relatively late in the day, in 1966, principally to ride the new 500 cc

BIKES

machine against Giacomo Agostini on the MV Agusta, but
this fast and furious duel at the top end of the racing ladder is
covered later in the book.

Mr Honda

The man who had the greatest influence on modern motor
cycling never set out to make himself famous. In the devasta-
tion of war-torn Japan, Mr Soichiro Honda was already forty
years old when he came across a consignment of 500 war-
surplus small two-stroke engines which had been used by the
Japanese army to power communications equipment. An
engineer and technician with some inventive flair, Mr Honda
saw their commercial possibilities and bought them all. In
those early post-war years, life in Japan was chaotic. There
was little public transport and hardly any fuel for private cars.
Honda set about adapting the small two-stroke engines for
use on bicycles. He cleared a bombsite, put up a small shack
as a workshop and with one ancient machine tool, an old
belt-driven lathe, a couple of salvaged desks and chairs, and a
few helpers, started what was to become the greatest motor-
cycle-manufacturing empire the world has ever known.

He always preferred to be in the background and, even
when his company had become famous throughout the world,
he was always happiest when beavering away on a difficult
technical problem in the corner of his factory. In a white coat
and neat hat – standard uniform for all Honda employees –
he was indistinguishable from any other Honda mechanic. Mr
Honda was not activated by a driving sense of mission,
purpose or calling. He was simply a shrewd and intelligent
businessman with a knack for picking good associates. He had
the Japanese capacity for hard work and persistence and,
above all, he had a quiet yet passionate desire to see his own
business prosper.

His father was first a blacksmith, and later owned a cycle
shop. Soichiro was born in the small rural village of Komyo,
near the city of Hamamatsu, in 1906. Scholastically he did not
impress. He hated examinations. Working with his hands

40

gave him the greatest delight. By the time he was sixteen he was working in an automobile-repair shop in Tokyo and after surviving the famous earthquake of 1923, which devastated seven square miles of the capital and killed 142,000, he began repairing cars that had been damaged in the tragedy.

At twenty-two he had his own garage business and raced cars in his spare time. Later he raced motor cycles. With hardly any knowledge of the business he later still set up as a manufacturer of piston rings and learned so quickly and thoroughly that within two years he was supplying parts to extremely exacting standards to 'big-name' customers. After the war the piston-ring business was sold at a handsome profit. Then came the new business of fitting his war-surplus engines to bicycles. When the supply ran out he began making his own engines. This led to the formation, in September 1948, of the Honda Motor Company Limited, which had a capital of around £900. It had 34 employees, but Mr Honda's ambition was limitless. In August 1949 Honda became the first post-war Japanese motor-cycle manufacturer to make its own engine and its own frame. Honda's first four-stroke machine was introduced in 1951. In 1952 the Honda Cub was an instant success, 6,500 being produced in the first seventeen months. A year later Honda held 70 per cent of the total Japanese market for clip-on units. The first exports were registered in 1957 – just two machines to Okinawa. Then came the introduction in 1958 of the 50 cc Super Cub. That same year two machines were exported to the United States and the first Honda machines arrived in Britain.

By 1962, with racing success boosting their technical brilliance and marketing flair, Honda sales reached £59 million and more than 65,000 Hondas were sold in the United States alone. Total production of Honda motor cycles had by 1968 exceeded ten million and the one-millionth sale was registered in the United States. By changing the image of motor cycling, Honda created a totally new market and in so doing established a whole new industry.

One of nine children, the man whose company was by now the largest manufacturer in the entire history of motor cycling was very much a home-spun industrialist. He shunned membership of corporate bodies and trade liaisons, much preferring to sort problems out within his own company. He found his own opportunities and dictated the course of his own business.

The little man not only revolutionised motor cycling throughout the world, but he turned bike racing upside-down as well. Never before had grand-prix racing been so vibrant, so exciting. But it was only a means to an end, and for Mr Honda business always came first. When he felt that racing would no longer further his business aims, he packed it in. His knack for pinpointing public needs and his ability to foresee trends was always a strong Honda characteristic. As long ago as the mid-1960s he predicted the age of customised motor cycles and present-day pollution problems. He was courageous too. Twice in its early years the Honda company tottered on the verge of collapse, but Mr Honda's faith in his company never wavered and the business was kept going.

When Mr Soichiro Honda made his first tentative visit to the Isle of Man to see the TT Races in 1954 he moved around unknown in the crowds, returning home disappointed and dejected because European racing machines were so much in advance of Honda models. Twenty years later, having retired as president of the company he founded, Mr Honda visited the Isle of Man again as part of a farewell world tour. Well within that time-span the Honda Motor Company had become a gigantic force in motor cycling, claiming for its new image a worldwide acceptance totally unheard-of by any other motor-cycle company in the past.

Yet he remained unchanged. For all his company's astronomic success, few would recognise the man who started it all. Indeed, hundreds of thousands of enthusiastic Honda riders throughout the world – were you to ask them – would not even know that a Mr Soichiro Honda ever existed.

50 cc Racing

Recognition with full world-championship status was granted to 50 cc racing in 1962. It came with the emergence of the

Japanese factories as the dominant force in grand-prix racing. Ernst Degner was the first-ever 50 cc world champion, with four wins in a row: Isle of Man, Holland, Belgium and Germany. He took the title for Suzuki by a margin of five points. But the honour of winning the first-ever round in 50 cc world-championship racing goes to Hans-Georg Anscheidt, who took his German Kreidler machine to an exciting win at Barcelona in the Spanish Grand Prix.

Anscheidt, who was born in East Prussia in 1935, began his career in cross-country events and later rode on grass, cinder and sand tracks. He had his first opportunity to ride a Kreidler machine whilst working for the factory in the testing and development department and secured the 50 cc European Championship in 1961. Only 5ft 2in tall and weighing about 9½ stone, he had the ideal stature for lightweight machine racing.

During the 1960s it was the Suzuki factory riders who gained most honours in 50 cc world-championship racing. They won the title six times between 1962 and 1969. Hugh Anderson (in 1963 and 1964) and Anscheidt (in 1967, 1968 and 1969) were responsible for Suzuki's impressive record and only in 1965, when Ralph Bryans took the title, did Honda ever achieve success in the class. However, they did it in typically sensational style with an incredible machine which, though only a 50 cc twin with tiny cylinders, scaled new heights for a racing bike. It had ten gear ratios, gave 13 bhp and was capable of travelling in excess of 100 mph. But as the 1960s drew to a close, the Japanese effort was largely spent in 50 cc racing and Spain's Angel Nieto on the Derbi factory machine was ready to take over. They were an unbeatable combination in 1969 and 1970, and again in 1972. Later that decade, through the initiative and drive of the factory's Dutch importer Henk Van Veen, the Kreidler factory gained further distinctions with the Van Veen Kreidler machines of Jan de Vries (who had gained the title on a Kreidler machine in 1971) and Henk Van Kessell winning the 50 cc world titles in 1973 and 1974. Nieto came back strongly to win the title on a Kreidler in 1975 and with Bultaco machinery in 1976 and 1977. Spain's Ricardo Tormo gave Bultaco their third successive 50 cc world championship in 1978, but with the small Spanish company grossly in debt and its future in the balance, the way was open for Kreidler to move in once more in 1979, the West German factory securing the world title that year through Italy's Eugenio Lazzarini.

Though there is obviously a place for the racing of lightweight machines in the world championships, they cannot compare in prestige or public appeal with the heavier-machine classes. After Honda had made their major effort in the early 1960s, they decided to pull out of 50 cc racing (and also the 125 cc class) after 1966 and Suzuki's interest in the class also waned. But despite these withdrawals, the class consolidated its place within the racing calendar. The FIM restrictions on 50 cc racing – only single-cylinder engines and no more than six-speed gearboxes – were introduced for 1969 when Nieto took the title by a single point from the Dutch rider Aalt Toersen on a Kreidler. The changes were designed to encourage some of the smaller factories to support 50 cc racing, and in 1969 the small Dutch concern of Jamathi, along with Derbi and Kreidler, all fielded works riders. Jan de Vries's world title in 1971 was secured at the final grand prix of the season, at the Jarama circuit in Spain, and by just one point. It was between the Dutchman and Angel Nieto, but the Spaniard came off in a battle to get in front, leaving de Vries to win the race and his first world title.

Some indication of the technical brilliance of the modern 50 cc machine came in 1973 when, despite the restrictions imposed by the FIM, the brilliantly tuned single-cylinder Van Veen Kreidlers were lapping in excess of 100 mph in the Belgian Grand Prix, and down the Masta straight in the same race, Jan de Vries's machine was reputed to be travelling at around 125 mph!

With six world championships to his credit in 50 cc racing, the Spaniard Angel Nieto is clearly the most successful rider in the class. He was born in Madrid in 1947 and by the time he was fourteen was working in the racing department of the famous Bultaco factory in Barcelona. But with Bultaco already fully committed to established riders, the ambitious Nieto could find no place in their race team, so he moved to the rival Derbi factory, who loaned him works machines for 1962. The following year, when only sixteen, he became an official works rider, finishing fifth in the Spanish and German Grands Prix. After that first world title in 1969, he was champion again in 1970, second in 1971, and champion again in 1972. Derbi's retirement from full competition in the world championships left him without a competitive ride, and after two disappointing years on Morbidelli machines, he bought the Van Veen Kreidler raced successfully by Henk Van Kessell and Jan de Vries in 1973 and 1974, to become successful once more, gaining world titles in both years.

Angel Nieto at one time flirted with motor racing and has cast an ambitious eye over the heavier, more prestigious bike classes. He has also been significantly successful in 125 cc racing, gaining world titles in 1971, 1972 and 1979. His uninhibited riding in the early days has been tempered by experience in more recent years, though he always rides strongly to win, getting close to the limit on numerous occasions.

FOUR

Japanese Factories Dominate Racing

I was lucky being at the peak of my career when motor-cycle racing was more vivid, exciting, rewarding and prosperous than at any time in its history. Grand-prix racing was at its best in the 1960s when the Japanese factories fought one another and poured huge sums of money into their respective bids to dominate the world championships. They undoubtedly produced the best bikes, but Britain still had the best riders. I'm not sure why we don't produce riders of world class any more. Maybe it's a hangover from the decline of the British motorcycle industry, but whatever the reason, the records over the last ten to fifteen years make sad reading if you are a British bike fan and can remember the 1960s. During that decade British riders won a total of fifteen world championships and Phil Read, Bill Ivy, myself and others like Bob McIntyre and John Hartle – and, of course, John Surtees in the early years – were the core of grand-prix racing in all except the lightweight classes. In the 1970s only seven world titles were won by British riders and the only new talent to emerge at international level was Barry Sheene. It's a mystery to me that we seem to produce a lot of promising riders who seldom travel further than homeland circuits. Maybe factory contracts are not as plentiful as they used to be, though in the 1960s there was fierce competition for those that were available. Perhaps sponsors don't invest like they used to. Whatever the reason, it's disappointing to see so many continental riders able to make regular trips from one grand prix to another and so many British riders content to stay at home.

One thing I'm pretty sure about is that the topliners today don't ride as hard as we used to in the 1960s. Then you had to ride to the limit of your bike's power and adhesion and your own abilities to win races. Today I get the impression that

46

although speeds have risen because of machine development, most riders keep well within the limits. They fall off through lack of concentration and by committing simple, basic errors at high speed, not because they are riding beyond the limit. That's the difference. Of the modern riders I have seen, the American Freddy Spencer comes nearest to the way we used to ride. He really goes for the results and if at times he looks a bit hairy, you certainly can't blame him for lack of trying.

One of the most fearless riders of my day was the diminutive Bill Ivy. He loved the good life and the glamorous trappings of being a successful contract rider in the 1960s. He had a big car, a London flat, plenty of girlfriends, and enjoyed a lifestyle in keeping with Britain's 'swinging sixties' image. Flamboyant off a motor cycle, he was pure dynamite racing one, and his sole world championship in the 125 cc class in 1967 did not begin to do justice to his enormous courage and talent.

That was the year Yamaha made a strong bid for honours in the 125 cc and 250 cc classes with Bill and Phil Read under contract. It was the factory's second major effort to make their mark in these classes. In 1964, after Jim Redman on the Honda had been untouchable in both categories, Yamaha and Suzuki developed new and exotic machines at enormous expense. For three years the rivalry between the three Japanese factories made grand-prix racing more vibrant, exciting and colourful than at any time in the past. Honda spent lavishly on their quest for success in 1964, but despite all their efforts Suzuki gained the 50 cc title through New Zealander Hugh Anderson while Phil Read, on a comparatively conventional Yamaha, took the 250 cc crown, beating Jim Redman on the Honda by just four points. Honda dominated the 350 cc class, with Jim Redman an easy world champion, and in the 500 cc class I had few problems and little real competition in taking the championship for the third year running, riding the MV Agusta.

In 1965, Honda's persistence in the 50 cc class paid off and the Irish rider Ralph Bryans brought them the title, with Luigi Taveri, also on a Honda, in second place. Suzuki, through Hugh Anderson, were relegated to third place. The seesawing continued, for Suzuki struck back to take the 125 cc title from Honda. Anderson rode a new water-cooled, disc valve twin which had a remarkable performance and this dynamic little Suzuki was much superior to the Hondas. It was a chastening experience for Honda in this class. Their best performance came from Taveri, who ended the season way down in fifth position, behind the Suzukis of Hugh Anderson and Frank Perris and the MVs of Derek Woodman and Ernst Degner.

The best racing was seen in the 250 cc class where a titanic struggle was anticipated between Jim Redman on the Honda and Phil Read on the Yamaha. In the end it was fairly easy for Yamaha after Read had won the first five rounds in the United States, West Germany, Spain, France and in the Isle of Man. Honda made a fight of it with Redman winning in Holland, Belgium and East Germany, but when Read responded with further wins in Czechoslovakia and Northern Ireland the battle was over. Redman ended the season in third position, trailing behind the Yamahas of Phil Read and the Canadian Mike Duff.

Redman had to fight unusually hard in the 350 cc class after MV Agusta entered the fray with brand-new three-cylinder machines which were leaner, quicker and handled better than the previous, more ponderous four-cylinder models, and were altogether highly competitive. They also introduced a new Italian rider called Giacomo Agostini, who rode with me for the first time in the MV Agusta team, in both 350 cc and 500 cc races. Bad luck robbed Ago of the 350 cc title at his first attempt. He won in West Germany, Finland and Italy (the third victory before an ecstatic 'home' crowd), and had convincing third places in the Isle of Man and in Holland. Redman won in the Isle of Man, and in Holland, East Germany and Czechoslovakia. Agostini needed to win the final round in Japan, but a broken contact breaker spring put him out of the running. It was a humiliating experience for the Japanese as I went on to win the race on the MV Agusta, but Jim Redman's second place (against Agostini's fifth) was enough to give him the title by just six points. Again in the 500 cc class there was no real opposition to MV Agusta. I won enough rounds to give me the title and Agostini finished ten points behind in second place. It was the fourth year running I had taken the 500 cc world championship and MV Agusta had now been unbeatable in the class since 1956, except for 1957 when Gilera took the title.

Honda's ambition was higher than ever and they decided to go for all five solo classes in 1966, in an enormous bid for world-championship glory. I had become bored with racing against the clock and my own best times on the 500 cc MV and was ready for a change, so when Jim Redman asked me to switch to Honda for the new season I was definitely interested. I was desperately in need of more competitive rides and had not really been able to get Count Agusta to take much interest in other classes. All his effort and energy were directed to the 500 cc bikes and, with Agostini being an Italian, it would be natural for him (should he make the grade) to take over in due course as the Italian factory's top rider. With Honda I would have the chance of competing in the 250 cc, 350 cc and 500 cc classes and for the most progressive factory in the world. Money came into it, too. If you're going to risk your neck racing you might as well do it for the best money you can get. I told Honda what I wanted and they didn't argue. I had desperately wanted to ride for Honda back in 1964 when my old friend Jim Redman tried to get the Honda bosses interested. When they flatly turned down the idea I was hurt and angry. In those days you didn't get a second chance of upsetting Honda and I had a black mark against my name from 1961, when I won the 250 cc world title on a 'loaned' Honda against the official works team (bad enough in itself), and then preferred to ride for MV Agusta in 1962. Derek Minter committed a similar 'crime' by beating the official riders in the 1962 TT and was never forgiven for it, later being ignored on more than one occasion when a Honda factory ride would have seemed obvious.

I was particularly put out when Jim tried to get me a ride in the 1964 Italian Grand Prix and Honda turned the idea down without giving any reason, for he had a lot of influence with Honda's top racing officials and for a long time ran the team very much as he wanted. The first glimmer that Honda might be interested came in 1965 when I received a letter offering me a ride in the Japanese Grand Prix at the end of the season. Still under contract to MV, I had to get Count Agusta's permission and that took some doing, but eventually he agreed and I rode the 250 cc Honda to victory before a Japanese crowd. I suppose that this win, supported by 350 cc and 500 cc wins at the same meeting in Japan on the MVs, made me a good candidate at a time when Honda needed to strengthen their team to contest their extended race programme.

So I signed for Honda and those historic battles between Honda and MV Agusta; Japan and Italy, Hailwood and Agostini, during 1966 and 1967 in the most prestigious class of all, were set to begin. For 1966 Honda kept the 1965 50 cc, 125 cc and 250 cc machines, enlarged the 250 to 296 cc for 350 cc competition, and brought out their new 500 cc four-cylinder model. Despite this monumental effort Suzuki sneaked ahead to take the 50 cc title through Hans-Georg Anscheidt, who was just two points ahead of Honda's Bryans and Taveri in second and third place at the end of the season. MV Agusta took the 500 cc title yet again by just six points. The Swiss rider Luigi Taveri did the job for them in the lightweight class and I beat Phil Read (Yamaha) on the 250s and Giacomo Agostini (MV Agusta) in the 350 cc class. On the 500 cc Honda I was six points short of Ago's total at the end of the season, but long before then I had wondered just what I had let myself in for, riding the big Honda. It was a brute of a machine, with immense power, but the frame was diabolical. Despite my protests during 1966 and 1967, Honda never did much to put it right. They were all for giving machines more power, but seemed to have a blind spot when it came to appreciating the deficiencies in the frame. I'm convinced nobody at Honda realised how difficult the 500 was to handle. In comparison the MV Agusta was docile. Another problem was that it just couldn't be trusted. Sometimes, when it started going in all directions, you could wind it on a bit more and you'd be all right. But not always . . . and then you were in trouble. Anyway, at the start of the season I wasn't too concerned because I knew Jim Redman would have prior claim on the best of the two big Hondas. He didn't disguise the fact that, as he was approaching the end of his career, a 500 cc world championship would nicely round off his racing ambitions, and who was I to argue, even though the Honda bosses recruited me specifically to bring them the 500 cc title?

We couldn't have started the 1966 season more success-fully. At Hockenheim Redman beat Agostini to win the 500 cc round and I beat the Italian in the 350 cc race. In the 250 cc class, I won, with Redman runner-up. At the Dutch Grand Prix I again won the 250 cc and 350 cc races and, despite having to ride a very poor second-string machine in the 500, I thought I might even win when at one point I was leading both Redman and Agostini. But then I came off and landed on my backside! We went to Belgium for the next round. For the past four years I had won the 500 cc race at the renowned and incredibly fast Spa circuit on the MV and nobody likes to play second fiddle where once you have been king. I really needed some points if I was going to make an impression at all on the 500 cc table, for Agostini at this stage was ahead, Jim Redman was in second place and I was losing touch in third place. I was well ahead of the field when it began to rain heavily and conditions were appalling. I was already thinking how stupid it was to race in such weather when Redman fell off and broke an arm. I might have gone on to win and, in the end, that would have made all the difference to the outcome of that year's 500 cc world championship, but I made up my mind and decided to call it a day. With the circuit swamped, I cruised into the pits and Agostini went on to win.

Jim's injury kept him out of racing for the remainder of the season, though he tried to race again in Northern Ireland towards the end of it, so it was now left to me to take up the challenge in the 500 cc class. I won in Czechoslovakia, the Isle of Man and in Northern Ireland. Agostini won in Finland, but his earlier performance on the MV Agusta had put him in an almost unassailable position. I was now riding in all three machine classes and having clinched the 250 cc and 350 cc world titles by the time we prepared for the final 500 cc grand prix at Monza, there was a chance of adding a third if I could beat Ago in Italy. It looked a possibility as I chased the

51

Italian, but then the Honda's valves buckled and Ago raced on to win and take the championship.

There was fierce battling again in 1967, though now Redman was retired (his injured arm never fully regained its strength and mobility for racing). Costs of racing were going through the roof as the Japanese factories piled on the pressure, but the first signs of collapse came with Honda's decision to pull out of 50 cc and 125 cc racing completely in 1967. It looked for a time as if their whole racing programme might be in doubt, but they finally agreed to give support to myself and Ralph Bryans in the three bigger machine classes. Suzuki were also feeling the financial strain and only Yamaha of the Japanese 'big three' were prepared to increase their investment in racing. Suzuki had an easy run in the 50 cc class, Anscheidt taking the title, with Katayama in second place and Stuart Graham, son of the first-ever 500 cc world champion in 1949, Les Graham, taking third place, both on Suzuki machines. In the 125 cc class, Bill Ivy was a worthy world champion on the Yamaha. Phil Read, also on a Yamaha, finished second and Graham gave Suzuki third place. In the 350 cc class I beat Agostini with reasonable comfort, but racing in the 250 cc and 500 cc classes could not have been closer. With all the races run, Phil Read and I had 50 points each in the 250 cc championship, and Agostini and I had 46 points each in the 500 cc class. The 250 cc title was mine because I had won five rounds against Phil's four, but on the 500s, Agostini and I each had five wins to our credit. The title went to the rider with the most second places – and that was Ago. He retained the title with second places in Holland, Czechoslovakia and Canada. I had finished second in Belgium and Italy.

Despite all their investment, effort and ambition, Honda had failed to win the solo championship which meant more than any other in terms of prestige and showroom sales, but for my part I never felt that I couldn't beat Ago, given equal machinery. The Italian's great strength was his consistency, and with the MV Agusta he had the more reliable machine in our epic duels in 1965 and 1966, but he was a worthy champion and became the most successful motor-cycle racer of all time in terms of results, with a remarkable record of fifteen world championships.

By 1968 it was obvious that the grand-prix merry-go-round was slowing down. The pulsating days of intense Japanese inter-factory rivalry, with the rich rider contracts being negotiated direct with headquarter chiefs back in Japan, were at an end. Honda cut back even further. Bryans and myself were given the go-ahead to race the current machines, but only in non-title races, and we had to make our own arrangements for looking after the bikes. Grand-prix racing was at an end for Honda. Suzuki took a similar decision, despite introducing an interesting new four-cylinder 125 cc bike at the end of 1967. Only Yamaha showed any enthusiasm to continue the fight. The way was now clear for Agostini on the MV Agusta and he romped home in both the 350 cc and 500 cc classes, winning all seventeen races! Anscheidt, who had been allowed to continue racing in the world championships by Suzuki, but at his own expense, took the 50 cc class, and only in the 125 cc and 250 cc classes was there any real interest, and this centred on the increasing rivalry between Bill Ivy and Phil Read, the Yamaha team mates. Yamaha dominated the results, with Read winning both championships and Ivy finishing second in each class. The 250 cc series was a superb cliff-hanger, and after the final grand prix in Italy, each rider had 52 points. It became even more exciting as it was quickly deduced that Read and Ivy had won five races each and also had two second places to their credit. The decision was finally made on the basis of best times, and Phil Read was declared World Champion.

By 1969 the racing scene had changed dramatically. The Japanese had lost interest in Europe and were directing their efforts increasingly to the vast potential market of North America. In the 350 cc and 500 cc classes Agostini continued undisturbed on the MV Agustas, again winning every grand prix in which he competed, to take both titles. Yamaha's absence from 125 cc and 250 cc racing gave new names on different machines a chance for the first time in years. Dave Simmonds took the 125 cc title on a Kawasaki, though the Japanese factory did precious little to support the British

53

rider's efforts, and Kel Carruthers, the Australian who was later to take over the management of the Yamaha international race team, became the 250 cc World Champion riding an Italian Benelli machine. The closest-fought battle was for 50 cc honours and in this class the FIM had brought in new regulations which meant that only single-cylinder machines with not more than six-speed gearboxes were eligible. The ruling had been intended to curb the Japanese bewildering race for more cylinders, but by the time the regulations came into force, the factories they had meant to discipline had left the scene. The Spaniard Angel Nieto, then new to grand-prix racing, took the title on the remarkably quick Derbi machine. He finished one point ahead of the Dutchman Aalt Toersen who rode a West German Kreidler.

But where was Hailwood in all this? With Honda's retirement my active interest had once more turned to cars – though I continued to follow closely the fortunes of two-wheel racing.

Riding to Team Orders

Riding to team orders is against the spirit of racing. That is the official line taken by the Federation Internationale Motorcycliste, the international ruling body of the sport, and who can argue against it? Yet I understand the attitude of manufacturers when they have a couple of riders fighting it out in a race. If they both go hell-bent for the line, they could fall off or blow up costly and elaborate machinery needlessly. Geoff Duke, I believe, had stronger views, stating openly that from a manufacturer's point of view riding to team orders was essential.

In 1968 this fundamental issue might well have cost Bill Ivy a world title. He and Yamaha team mate Phil Read were at loggerheads after racing brilliantly in 1967, when Ivy won the 125 cc world championship and Read finished second in both the 125 cc and 250 cc classes. Honda pulled out of racing by 1968 and Yamaha had things much their own way in both classes. Track rivalry between the two factory riders led to

keen early-season racing, but after Ivy's sensational performances on the Isle of Man, when he became the first rider ever
to lap the famous Mountain Circuit at 100 mph on a 125 cc
machine, there were murmurings that the results were
perhaps not quite what they seemed, and that the pair were
riding to some kind of factory-dictated racing pattern; but
while things were going well, and the racing thrilled and
entertained the crowds, did it really matter?

It certainly mattered in Czechoslovakia. An angry Bill Ivy
dragged everything out into the open after Read had won the
250 cc race. He claimed that the Yamaha plan was for Phil to
win the 125 cc title, leaving Ivy to take the 250 cc crown. Read
retorted: 'I ride to win or quit.' The feud deepened as the
season progressed. Read, too, acknowledged the existence of
a team plan when defending his own position, arguing that
now that Yamaha had succeeded in winning the manufacturer's class of the championship, he considered it was every
man for himself.

Ivy countered by saying that he had let Read win the 125 cc
title, so Read should now let him win the 250 cc championship. 'I fell off in Czechoslovakia because I slowed down
to follow him,' Ivy claimed. 'I only wish this business had
happened earlier in the year. Then we'd have found out who
was the better rider.'

The rift widened at the Ulster Grand Prix. The original plan
was for both riders to contest only the 250 cc event and Read
was alleged to have submitted entries for himself and Ivy on
that basis. Race secretary Bill McMaster subsequently re-
ported that there had been a telephone call from Bill stating
that Phil had no authority to fix his starts, and that he wanted
to compete in the 125 cc race as well. When Read heard about
this, he also filed his entry for the 125 cc race.

In the meantime the FIM warned Phil Read at a prior grand
prix in Finland that the international rules of racing required
riders to make a genuine effort and that any action directing a
rider not to win races was illegal under FIM rules. But by this
time, with Yamaha on the verge of racing retirement, the
riders were thinking only of their own reputations. Read won
both races in Finland. Ivy collected all the points in Northern

Ireland. In the final grand prix in Italy, Ivy beat Read in the 125 cc race, though Read had already made sure of the title with six wins out of the nine races. The crucial 250 cc round was run in an atmosphere of open hostility between the two riders. If Read won, he would be double world champion. If Ivy lost he would be left with nothing. Phil led at the start, with Bill close behind. In an effort to overtake, Ivy was racing very near the limit. Phil was dismayed as his machine faltered, but by this time Bill's Yamaha had mechanical problems and in the end he had difficulty finishing in second place.

The result gave both riders the same number of total points and they each had the same number of second places. Phil Read took the title because his timings were better than Ivy's. Bill protested, alleging a technical infringement, but the objection was overruled.

It isn't surprising that the public hate the idea of team tactics. They pay their money to see a race and expect every rider to go as hard as he can to win. Many riders, however, see the sense in manufacturers having a say in the way the game should be played. The factories spend enormous sums of money designing, building and developing highly complex and sophisticated race machinery, and to let riders become dictators, often for self-glorification, is considered economic nonsense. Even in motor-cycle racing, the old saying that he who pays the money calls the tune can't be ignored, though some riders find it hard to accept. Bob McIntyre was very much an individualist and loathed riding to orders as a member of the Honda team in the 1960s. The brilliant Derek Minter never submitted to team discipline, and the great and legendary Stanley Woods left the all-conquering Norton works team in the 1930s because he was instructed *not* to win the 1933 Ulster Grand Prix.

MV . . . and the Count

Agostini and Count Agusta were a devastating combination. In just seven years they together secured twelve world championships. They have been criticised and devalued for it, because they faced little real opposition. I was always confident myself that I could outride Ago on equal machinery, and I didn't always see eye to eye with the Count. But you can't take that enormous achievement from them, whatever the circumstances. All those races still needed winning. When the rest of the Italian factories pulled out of racing at the end of 1957, it was on the cards that MV would follow. The Count decided to soldier on and in the 1960s and early 1970s I believe that he and Agostini, virtually on their own, maintained the status of the 500 cc class.

Giacomo Agostini made his road-racing debut on a 175 cc Morini when just 18 and finished second to the Italian champion in his first race. He was Italian 500 cc champion four years later and in 1965 won his first grand prix in Germany on the MV 3. From then it was success all the way, and in terms of results he quite easily became the most successful world-championship racer of all time. In Italy he was a national hero and his traditional good looks, Latin temperament and flashing smile brought him film and modelling engagements and repeated requests to endorse products. Ago got on well with Count Agusta and if in their long association there were disagreements, none broke the surface until the latter years when Phil Read's influence on Count Agusta forced him away to ride for Yamaha.

Ago was one of the earliest critics of the Mountain Circuit on the Isle of Man, claiming it was too dangerous for modern racing. He first raced on the Island in 1965, finishing third in the Junior TT and retiring in the Senior. He won ten TTs in an outstanding record which included four Senior-Junior TT doubles. After his close friend Gilberto Parlotti was killed there in 1972 he refused to ride on the Isle of Man again and his criticism of the course obviously contributed ultimately to its downfall as a grand-prix circuit. He was only 5ft 5in tall, but he could handle the big MVs well. He was a safe rider, conventional in style, and extremely consistent. He won the Belgian Grand Prix, the fastest race in the world-championship calendar, eight times running, and for four years in succession won the 350 cc and 500 cc races in East Germany.

For a while we raced as team mates, but when I switched to Honda he took over as MV's top rider and for two years we battled for the 500 cc crown. It was a head-on fight at one grand prix after another, and although you can't afford to be too charitable to other riders in motor-cycle racing, the rivalry was good-humoured enough and we got on well together. There was much more needle when Phil Read and Agostini rode as rivals some years later. The Italian resented the way Phil took advantage of his crash in Italy, and his resultant lack of form, to stake his claim for a contract with Count Agusta. Read took the championship from him in 1973, after seven years of continuous success, and retained it in 1974. But by this time Ago had stormed off to join Yamaha with the avowed intention of taking the title back from Read and MV, and thumbing his nose at them into the bargain. He did just that in 1975 in a very creditable performance. It couldn't have been easy switching to the Yamaha two-stroke after years of racing the MV four-strokes and by that time he must have been thirty-two. He took the title from Read by a margin of eight points, winning in France, Germany, Finland and Italy. Appropriately his final rides at the end of his career were back on the MV, and at Assen, in the Dutch Grand Prix of 1976, he won the 350 cc race in convincing style. In the final round that year at the Nurburgring, Agostini elected to ride the MV instead of the Suzuki he had ridden earlier in the season and, in what was effectively the last international success for both Agostini and MV Agusta, led for the entire seven laps.

At a time when it was fashionable in the 1960s for riders to express themselves strongly in public and to fight hard for a better deal with factories and circuit authorities, Agostini was relatively easy-going and seldom fell out with anyone, even his boss. That was more than I could do, for Count Domenico Agusta was difficult and unpredictable and at times totally unreasonable. More than once I lost my temper with him, yelled back at his accusations and walked out of his office. But, for all that, he could be charming, charitable and friendly. He was very much an individual and he ran MV Agusta autocratically. He didn't know the meaning of delegation and he made all the decisions. In many ways he was an astute businessman, but he invested a fortune in motor-cycle racing with little reward other than the pleasure of seeing Italy and his own company the most successful in the world. It was almost impossible to get to know him intimately. Of the British riders he had under contract, perhaps Les Graham was taken most into his confidence. He was passionately interested in racing, yet seldom attended race meetings, and he was obsessed with the success of his own factory. When his machines were beaten or other things went wrong he could get very angry. He was a prodigious worker and virtually all his time was spent at the MV Agusta works at Gallarate. He was really only interested in the world championships and in any major Italian meeting, and it used to annoy me that he would not permit me to ride the MV at British meetings. He had no conception of time, and expected everyone else to dedicate themselves, as he did, to the factory. I was not alone in flying from Britain to Italy specially for a meeting and then to be kept waiting, sometimes for hours on end, on one occasion, for several days.

Count Agusta started the habit of factories 'buying off' the opposition. At first he tried to win grand-prix races with Italian riders, but the best were already under contract and the remainder weren't good enough. When the Count wanted something passionately, as he did motor-cycle racing success, he didn't wait for it to happen. Often miserly in money matters, he would spend handsomely and impetuously when he wanted something badly enough. He lured riders like Les Graham, Tarquinio Provini, Ray Amm and Gary Hocking to MV with profitable contracts, doing riders a good turn in the process, for until then there had been a feeling, certainly in Britain, that you rode for the honour and not for the cash. He never used his outstanding racing successes commercially and although his son, Count Corrado Agusta, tried hard to make some economic sense out of the bike operation, the motor-cycling activities virtually ended when Count Agusta, within a few days of his sixty-fourth birthday, died in Milan in 1971 after a heart attack.

It became fashionable to play down the record-book statistics of Agostini and MV Agusta in the 1960s, but at times this attitude got out of hand as reporters and others seemed to criticise them for being there at all. The races were obviously too predictable and boring, but the championships would have been much worse off without the presence of Ago and MV.

As early as 1963, MV Agusta's dominance of the 500 cc grands prix irritated former World Champion Geoffrey Duke so much that he set up his own team to knock them off their perch. Duke had ridden for MV's rival Italian factory, Gilera, before their withdrawal from racing at the end of 1957 and had taken the world 500 cc title three years running on their superb multi-cylinder machines. The bikes were still stored in the factory and would doubtless give the MVs a good run for their money, for Count Agusta had not found it necessary to spend much time or money in developing the MVs. With little opposition they were quite good enough to win the championships as they were.

Having persuaded Gilera to release the famous machines, Duke signed Derek Minter and John Hartle to ride them under his management and the *Scuderia Duke* banner. At this time I was under contract to MV and had taken the world title on the 500 the year before. Minter particularly, and Hartle, were hard men to beat and were likely to be very fast indeed on the Gileras. They proved me right at Monza where both riders, during tests, were lapping at around 116 mph. It looked as though MV were going to be hard pressed for the first time in six years: and I was going to have a much tougher fight retaining the title than I had experienced in winning it. But Derek, though a magnificent rider, was seldom happy when riding in a team and even at Imola had protested that Hartle had been given the faster machine. Later he broke his back in a crash at Brands Hatch and although he recovered sufficiently to take his place on the Gilera again, a further disagreement with Geoffrey Duke didn't help. In the end Gilera, through Hartle, won in Holland with Phil Read (who had been drafted in to take over from the injured Minter) in second place. Hartle and Read were second and third in the Isle of Man and Read, Hartle and Minter were second in Belgium, Northern Ireland and East Germany respectively, but I was able in the end to win seven of the eight rounds to take the championship for the second year running, and by a much more comfortable margin than I had anticipated when Duke had first announced his plans.

But it was an enterprising move and had certainly added much-needed life and excitement to the class.

FIVE
By Vic Willoughby

How the Machines have Changed

From the start of the world championships in 1949 up to the present time, the technical development of grand-prix machines splits neatly into two distinct phases. First there was the gradual rise to dominance of the howling four-stroke multi, with more and more cylinders as time went by, latterly with four valves apiece. Second there was the relentless ascendancy of the petulant-sounding water-cooled two-stroke to a position of complete invincibility in all classes.

Both these trends were inevitable under the FIM's post-war formula of fixed engine capacities and no supercharging. Indeed, the FIM hastened the two-stroke's take-over when, at the end of 1969, it outlawed engines with more than four cylinders (for 350 and 500 cc), two cylinders (125 and 250 cc) and one cylinder (50 cc) – because the four-stroke had long relied on more and smaller cylinders (hence higher peak revs) for its edge over the two-strokes.

Yet neither avenue of development could have brought the success it did without the phenomenal achievements of the tyre boffins in providing the grip necessary to harness unprecedented engine power and permit undreamed-of cornering angles. Suspension developments, too, have contributed to high-speed roadholding, though this seems a less exact science and progress has been patchy.

Fascinating as that overall picture is, the details are even more so. Considering the four-stroke first, the British and Italian singles that won the lion's share of the titles in the first few years of the championships were living on borrowed time. In the last year or two of the European championships before the war, machines of that type had been emphatically de-throned by supercharged multis (both two-stroke and four-

62

stroke) in all classes. And it was only the post-war ban on supercharging that gave the singles their brief new lease of life.

Alas for Britain, her best 350 – the single-ohc Mark 8 KTT Velocette – was doomed to an early demise. Harold Willis, the factory's brilliant race engineer, had died suddenly of meningitis in the summer of 1939, since when Velocette design had stagnated. With no development whatsoever, the bikes were still good enough for two great but ageing pre-war stars to win the first two world championships – Freddie Frith in 1949 and Bob Foster the following year. But a conversion to twin overhead camshafts failed to make the progress it should have done, and the well-loved black-and-gold singles were soon outclassed by the double-knocker works Nortons.

Painstaking engine development under Joe Craig – including shorter strokes, bigger bores and outside flywheels – steadily boosted the power of both the 350 and 500 cc Nortons. At the same time handling was vastly improved by the adoption of Rex McCandless's so-called featherbed frame (with duplex loops and pivoted rear fork), while the graceful artistry of Geoff Duke also did much to nullify the extra speed of the Italian Gilera fours.

These three factors (improved power, handling and riding skill) combined to earn four manufacturers' titles for Norton (500 cc 1950 and 1951, 350 cc 1951 and 1952) and three individual titles for Duke (500 cc 1951, 350 cc 1951 and 1952). But it was a hopeless cause. And, in championship terms, the British single was laid to rest when, in 1953, Duke bowed to the inevitable and joined Gilera. There, in a fruitful liaison with race engineer Piero Taruffi, he suggested various modifications which made the big four much more raceworthy.

Narrowing the sump and exhausts enabled both the centre of gravity and overall height to be lowered. Braking power was increased by a change to twin leading shoes up front. A backrest on the seat and kneepads on the back of the tank helped improve the rider's control (those days he stayed in the seat when cornering). Wheel suspension was refined with twin-rate springs (Gilera had already abandoned the original girder front fork and rear torsion bars). The frame was stiffened, a fifth gear was added to the transmission, the rear tyre was fattened for extra cornering grip and various forms of streamlining were concocted, starting with a steering-head fairing and finishing with a full frontal 'dustbin'.

Simultaneously, the Arcore engineers boosted engine performance by enlarging the valves, widening their angle, stretching the bore, tailoring carburettor size between 25 and 32 mm to suit different circuits (they had switched from two carbs to four in 1951) and fitting exhaust megaphones. This wonderful teamwork made the 500 cc Gilera well-nigh invincible until the factory quit racing at the end of 1957. Duke romped to a hat-trick of individual titles in that class in 1953, 1954 and 1955, and Bob McIntyre, taking over in mid-season, helped the factory collar both manufacturers' titles (350 and 500 cc) in 1957.

The Gilera, however, was not the first multi to win a world championship. That distinction fell to the AJS Porcupine double-knocker parallel twin when Les Graham took the very first 500 cc title, in 1949. An ungainly machine, the Porcupine was designed by Joe Craig during the war, when there was no inkling that supercharging would be banned. For that reason it had a cradle on top of the integral four-speed gearbox that mystified most observers, though not the Duke of Edinburgh. When he saw the bike at the Earls Court Show in 1952, he pointed to the cradle and asked: 'What's that for – a supercharger?' Indeed, it was to have accommodated a gear-driven Roots-type blower, while the cylinders were installed horizontally, with deep spike finning on the one-piece head to catch the air and prevent overheating.

A most unusual feature of the original design was its induction layout. The pipe from the blower swept forward over the inlet cambox, then down to inlet ports which approached the valves from the opposite side to usual. The object was to get a straighter gas entry into the cylinders and minimise the amount of compressed gas blown out through the exhaust valves during the overlap phase.

As it turned out, the supercharging ban was announced before the engine could even be built in this form, so a fresh cylinder head had to be designed. In this the inlet ports approached the valves from the usual side. But though various induction layouts were tried, none of them gave free-enough breathing to lift peak revs beyond 7,600 rpm, whereas a double-ohc twin of 68.5 × 68 mm bore and stroke would have been expected to produce its best power at 9,000 rpm or more. In short, the Porcupine failed to adapt from the low-revving high-torque concept of the original design to the high-revver necessary for competitive power under post-war formula. Graham's title was its first and last.

The factory's 350 cc 7R, however (the so-called Boy Racer), played a prominent role in the rearguard action of the British single. For, although it never scaled world-title heights, it performed well for long enough to enable Reg Armstrong to take second place in the 1949 championship, followed by third places for Les Graham, Bill Doran, Rod Coleman and Mike Duff in 1950, 1951, 1954 and 1964 respectively – a remarkable record considering the ludicrously tight budget imposed on Jack Williams when he took over development in 1953.

In essence, the 7R started life (in 1948) as a pretty obvious copy of the Mark 8 KTT Velocette – except that the camshaft was driven by chain, not bevel gears; that the frame was a much lighter welded duplex-loop affair; and that the front fork was telescopic (not girder), while the rear fork was controlled by fat, poorly damped spring-and-hydraulic struts (nicknamed jampots) instead of the Dowty oleo-pneumatic struts on the Velo.

Fairly early in the Ajay's life (1952) a three-valve variant (the 7R3A, with two exhaust valves) was designed and showed considerable promise when Rod Coleman won the Junior TT after five successive Norton victories. Within a month, the 7R3B – with the camshafts driven by bevels instead of chain (so facilitating compression changes) – was bench-tested and nudged 40 bhp at 8,000 rpm. But the factory quit before it could be raced, after which the 7R continued only as a two-valve catalogue racer.

Though he would dearly have liked to switch to separate camshafts (indeed to more cylinders) had his brief permitted it, Williams knuckled down to boosting the engine's bmep (the punch of each individual power impulse) by extensive research into inlet port shapes, valve sizes, and squish areas in the combustion chamber giving a compact space and ultra-high compression ratio. He also pushed the peak revs safely up to 7,800 rpm by shortening the stroke, substantially increasing the initial valve acceleration to tame valve float and tailoring the cam form to suit the valve-spring characteristics, so eliminating spring failure.

Overall, Williams pushed the 7R's power up from 37 bhp at 7,500 rpm to nearly 42 at 7,800, while cutting its weight from 310 to 285 lb.

But it was the Italians who most fully exploited the racing single's potential. In the little Moto Guzzi race shop nestling on the eastern shore of Lake Como, the brilliant Ing Giulio Carcano developed 350 cc flat singles so light, slim and nimble that they made monkeys of the much more powerful Gilera fours and DKW threes by taking the individual titles from 1953 to 1957 inclusive, before Moto Guzzi, too, pulled out of racing.

Before 1953, Moto Guzzi's world-championship successes had been confined to the 250 cc class. But when, in 1952, Enrico Lorenzetti clinched their third title in the four years of the series, after Fergus Anderson had won their seventh 250 cc TT, they decided to stretch the engine capacity and try their luck in the 350 cc division.

The first tentative move was to increase the cylinder dimensions from 68 × 68 mm to 72 × 80 mm (320 cc), and the result was nothing if not encouraging. On the old, ultra-fast Hockenheim loop, where speed was decisive, Anderson won the German Grand Prix, then chased home the works Nortons of Ray Amm and Ken Kavanagh in the Junior TT. Emboldened by those results, Carcano quickly built a full-size engine (75 × 79 mm) and Anderson promptly took over from Geoff Duke as world 350 cc champion in 1953.

From then on Carcano did a superb development job on those simple singles – curing the inevitable teething troubles as they arose and giving as much thought to every other aspect of the machines' performance as to engine power. Most noticeably, he pared weight relentlessly and safely to a remarkable 216 lb (98 kg), including the magnesium-alloy dustbin fairing, and dropped the centre of gravity (already very low because of the horizontal cylinder) to rock-bottom by putting the fuel tank just above the cylinder. This shrewd line of development gave the riders not only easier handling, later braking and faster cornering than their rivals, but also much more confidence in their mastery of the bike, so that they cornered consistently nearer the limit.

In engine development, Carcano put as much emphasis on torque as on power and supplemented his bench tests with track tests at Modena. He scorned telescopic forks in favour of leading links (with their lower unsprung weight, greater stiffness and more refined damping), switched from spine frame to space frame to suit the adoption of a dustbin fairing and produced one of such exquisite shape and small frontal area that 38 bhp at the rear wheel gave a top speed of 140 mph and an overall fuel consumption of 60-65 mpg.

No consideration was too insignificant in the quest for lightness: the fairing was unpainted; there were no inner valve springs; a 10 mm plug was used while 14 mm was the norm; dual ignition was dropped because the only magneto available (single-spark) was lighter than a battery, two coils and two contact breakers; the light-alloy cylinder bore was plated to save the weight of an iron sleeve; wherever feasible, aluminium was substituted for steel and magnesium for aluminium. And, as the weight plummeted, Carcano even dispensed with one of the duplex front brakes because the remaining one was amply powerful for the easier task. Fergus Anderson's second successive championship (1954), Bill Lomas's in 1955 and 1956 and Keith Campbell's in 1957 were akin to taking sweets from a child.

Yet Carcano was by no means blinkered in his outlook. Even while his featherweight flat singles were demonstrating the wisdom of the simple approach, he foresaw the time when, at least on the fastest circuits, he might need more power than he could squeeze from a single cylinder. The outcome was his most exciting engine – a water-cooled 500 cc V-eight. (A 350 cc version was made too but not raced.) And so fast did the race shop work that the engine was bench-tested, and the bike track-tested at Monza, within six months of the initial inspiration late in 1954.

Following a brace of practice sessions in 1955, and a race debut in the Imola Gold Cup meeting at Easter 1956, the V-eight caused palpitations in the Gilera camp at Solitude only three months later. There, in the German Grand Prix, Lomas on the eight and Duke on the Gilera romped away from the pack and swopped places for twenty-five minutes before the Gilera lost its sparks and the Moto Guzzi its water. Clearly the V-eight was already competitive and its promise was underlined by a simulated race test at Monza (Lomas was injured before the race itself, the Italian Grand Prix), a world 10 km record on the Appian Way, near Rome, early in 1957, followed by Dickie Dale's Gold Cup victory at Imola. Regrettably, the management's sudden decision to quit racing came before the bike could get into its full stride.

Inevitably, the 500 cc eight was considerably heavier than the 350 cc flat single. But, at 320 lb (145 kg), it was comparable to the rival fours and it had more power. The initial 64 bhp (at the rear wheel) at 12,000 rpm was quickly pushed up to 72 at 12,200, giving 175 mph on petrol on the Appian Way, and revised carburation boosted that to 80 bhp by the end of the summer.

Complex though it looked, with two banks of interlaced 20 mm Dellorto carburettors, the engine was such a model of compactness that the fairing was only 3 cm (1.2 in) wider than that of the 350 cc single. The forged crankshaft was short and stiff; the wet cylinder liners measured 44 × 41 mm bore and stroke; and the valves, operated by four overhead camshafts, were seated directly in the light-alloy heads. Engine oil was contained in the large-diameter frame spine; the rear fork pivoted in a massive lug on the back of the six-speed gearbox; and the twin-rate struts for the leading-link front fork were outside (not inside) the stanchions for quick experimental changes. The V-eight was robbed of a rosy future.

Moto Guzzi's sudden withdrawal from the world championships was orchestrated with those of Gilera (350 and 500 cc) and FB Mondial (125 and 250 cc). And the vacuum in the bigger classes was promptly filled by MV Agusta fours, on which (along with three-cylinder models in the late 1960s and early 1970s) John Surtees, Gary Hocking, Mike Hailwood, Giacomo Agostini and Phil Read netted 28 titles between them.

Right from the start the 500 cc MV four looked uncannily like the Gilera – which was hardly surprising since they both came from the drawing board of Ing Pietro Remor. Early on, however, the MV was distinctive in having torsion-bar springing at the front as well as the rear, and even more so in having shaft final drive – which necessitated a double rear fork in the form of a pivoted parallelogram to suit the action of the universal joints.

In the transition to conventional suspension and chain drive (under the influence of Les Graham, who joined them for 1951), MV flirted with a cumbersome Earles-type pivoted front fork of doubtful merit. They also changed from central to side plugs (which Gilera never did).

On the track, Graham had to wrestle with poor handling, uncertain gear selection and a speed deficit against the Gileras. But his performances in 1952 (Senior TT runner-up, Ulster lap record and wins in the Italian and Spanish grands prix) promised brighter results in 1953 (when the 500 was first partnered by the 350). Alas, fulfilment was delayed when Graham was killed early in the Senior TT, while lying second to Geoff Duke, and three years elapsed before Surtees joined the team and set them on the road to glory.

Besides his brilliant riding, Surtees's most fruitful contribution to the development of the fours was in the field of handling. So far as the engines were concerned, especially the smaller one, they were vulnerable to a serious challenge from a less antiquated design. The challenge came in 1962, when Honda bored out their world-beating 16-valve 250 cc four by a mere 3 mm to 285 cc (47 × 41 mm) for Jim Redman to win the world 350 cc championship – despite MV's acquisition of the incomparable Mike Hailwood, following Surtees's and Hocking's defection to car racing.

Stretched through 339 to 349 cc, the Honda four gave Redman a further three 350 cc titles on the trot by virtue of its lighter weight, slimmer dimensions and the greater power and mechanical safety alike bestowed by its paired valves.

MV's response in 1965 was to boost the power and reliability of their 350 by adopting four-valve heads, while slimming it by switching to three cylinders. But it was not good enough. Anyway, with Hailwood in their camp for 1966 and 1967, Honda again humiliated MV by stretching a winning 250 (their 24-valve six) to 297 cc for Mike to keep Agostini at bay.

In the 500 cc class, MV's old four had a longer run because Honda didn't make their challenge until 1966, when MV stretched Ago's three through 420 to 489 cc. Once Honda quit the championships in 1967, Ago and his three ruled the 350 and 500 cc divisions for five years. But in the early 1970s the challenge of the Yamaha twins and fours (especially Jarno Saarinen's) forced MV back to four cylinders (still with paired valves) for more power, though they managed to avoid any increase in width. They were the last four-strokes to hold the big titles – through Ago (350) in 1973 and Read (500) in 1974.

A bit less glamorous maybe, the lightweights that contested the championships before the Honda takeover in 1961 were nevertheless mostly beautifully engineered, high-revving Italian double-knocker singles from FB Mondial, MV Agusta, Moto Guzzi, Benelli and Moto Morini – though parallel twins, too, were fielded by MV and Mondial (250 cc) and by Gilera (125). The spectacular exception to this early Italian dominance came in 1953 and 1954 when NSU left everybody standing with their 125 cc Rennfox single and 250 cc Rennmax twin, both born of a failed 500 cc double-knocker four and both gaining an edge in handling from beam frames and leading-link forks.

With so much less power than the bigger bikes, the lightweights were not only first into windcheating but also went farthest, with large faired tails as well as frontal 'dustbins' (which were banned after 1957). But with big valves, long timings, high piston crowns and peak revs up to 11,000 rpm (250 cc) and 12,000 (125), the Achilles' heel of the lightweight single was valve float. A brief bout of overrevving and the valves would tangle with one another or the piston and put the bike on the sidelines.

NSU were among the first to tame valve float by accelerat-

Geoffrey Duke at Quarter Bridge on the first lap of the Junior T.T. I.o.M.
Duke brought Norton the 350cc and 500cc World Championship double
in 1951 and the 350cc World Championship the following year

20 year old Mike Hailwood on an MV Agusta at the Senior
International T.T. I.o.M.

John Hartle (left) who came second and Mike Hailwood (right) third congratulate John Surtees on winning the 1960 Senior T.T. I.o.M.

Mike Hailwood on his MV Agusta in the 1963 Ulster Grand Prix

Mike Hailwood (No. 5) chasing John Hartle (No. 4) in the Senior T.T. in 1963

Jim Redman (Honda, No. 7) and Mike Duff (AJS, No. 8) at the start of the 1965 Junior International T.T. I.o.M.

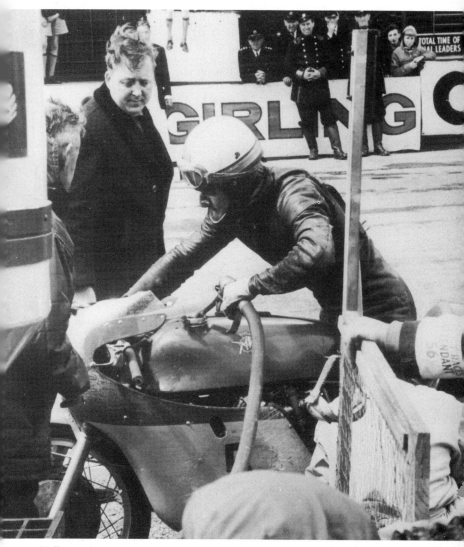

Hailwood helps himself to fuel in an effort to speed up a pit-stop in the
1965 Senior T.T. I.o.M.

Mike Hailwood wearing the laurels after winning the 500cc on his Honda at the 1966 Ulster Grand Prix

Hailwood racing at Oulton Park in 1967

Hailwood astride his Honda before the 500cc Senior T.T., I.o.M. 1967

Hailwood relaxing at home with some of his many trophies

Quitting at the top, Mike Hailwood in action before his retirement in
1968

Giacomo Agostini on an MV Agusta in 1968, the most successful road racer of all time. Agostini won a record five 350cc/500cc double World Championships 1968-72

Agostini at the 1977 German Grand Prix after his much publicised move to Yamaha in 1974

Mike Hailwood on the starting grid for his comeback race at the Isle of Man in 1978

Once learnt, never forgotten: Hailwood on the way to victory in the 1979 Senior T.T. I.o.M.

Celebrating his remarkable victory surrounded by fans

Donington 1978

Above & below:
On his 864 Ducati.

ing the valves fiercely for only about the first quarter lift, so giving the springs more time to arrest and reverse the motion. Indeed, so effective was this ploy that they were able to change the Rennfox engine from double overhead camshafts to a single shaft and rockers during its second title-winning year (1954, Ruppert Hollaus).

A few years later Ducati beat the valve-float problem entirely with their triple-camshaft desmodromic 125 cc single, in which return springs were abandoned and extra cams used to close the valves. Desmo engines were soon in great demand and Ducati built parallel twins of 125, 250 and 350 cc, and even designed a 125 cc four. But, once again, a management decision to pull out frustrated the race engineers when prospects looked rosy.

The simplest answer to valve float, however, was Honda's resurrection of the four-valve cylinder head, which had the additional advantages of better breathing, a much more compact combustion space (with squish segments front and rear for extra turbulence) and a shorter flame path from the central sparking plug.

Four-valve heads had been raced some 30 years earlier, notably on Rudge and Excelsior singles. But in those days the emphasis was on the thermodynamic benefits – better breathing and burning. Honda exploited the mechanical benefits, too, by using double overhead camshafts and tiny cylinders to slash reciprocating weights and so boost their peak revs safely to unprecedented heights.

Starting with a cylinder size of 62 cc (125 cc twin and 250 cc four), Honda quickly shed their initial image of being dependable but slow. In just two years, they gave track performance a new meaning and the world titles began to roll in. Between them, Tom Phillis, Mike Hailwood, Jim Redman, Luigi Taveri and Ralph Bryans collected 16 individual titles and 18 manufacturers', including all five solo classes in 1966.

As the two-stroke threat from Suzuki and Yamaha began to stiffen in the mid-1960s, so Honda countered by reducing cylinder size still more. The smallest was 25 cc (50 cc twin and 125 cc five), allowing peak revs of some 19,000 rpm, with the mechanical safety limit beyond the magic 20,000. Yet one of

71

Honda's closest shaves – before Phil Read's air-cooled Yamaha disc-valve twin ousted Redman's four from the 250 cc championship – came from an 'oldfashioned' four-stroke single. That was in 1963, when Tarquinio Provini narrowly failed to dethrone Redman on the low, light, slim and nimble 250 cc double-knocker Moto Morini, with an engine that revved reliably at a remarkable 11,000 rpm and produced an astonishing bmep of 206 psi at 10,500.

Honda's withdrawal in 1967 left the two-strokes well on the way to total supremacy. But when, twelve years later, Honda sought to recapture their former glory with the NR500, they seemed to have bitten off more than they, or any other four-stroke engineers, could chew. Not only had two-stroke power and reliability advanced enormously, but the FIM had meanwhile restricted engines to a maximum of four cylinders, so closing the path by which Honda had previously kept the four-stroke competitive.

The seeds of two-stroke supremacy were sown in the MZ race shop at Zschopau, East Germany. There, in the 1950s, Ing Walter Kaaden – convinced of the total dependence of the unblown two-stroke on natural resonances in the inlet and exhaust tracts – patiently developed a basic engine formula that was copied first by Suzuki and Yamaha, then by every other race shop that won a world title.

MZ themselves could have reaped the benefit of this work if Kaaden had not been hamstrung by a political regime that kept him pathetically short of materials and facilities and denied him the Western currency necessary to retain top riders once Ernst Degner had defected to the West in 1961.

The formula comprises a short, highly resonant induction tract controlled by a cutaway disc mounted on the crankshaft (this gives a long inlet phase without too-late port closure); an auxiliary transfer port (or ports) opposite the exhaust port, in addition to the main transfers at the sides; a large squish area in the combustion chamber; and a highly resonant exhaust system whose job is to scavenge the cylinder, pull in the gas from the crankcase and minimise the amount that sneaks out through the exhaust port.

True, Yamaha's titles from 1970 onward were won with

piston-controlled induction instead of the earlier disc valves that had taken Bill Ivy and Phil Read to the top in 1964, 1965, 1967 and 1968. But the switch was made for commercial, not technical reasons; and this attempt to make their racers look like their roadsters eventually necessitated the complication of shutters to vary the height of the exhaust ports and so broaden the spread of torque.

But MZ were not the first to worry the four-strokes in the world championships. While Kaaden pegged away in relative obscurity, Helmut Görg developed an odd-looking 350 cc DKW three in Ingolstadt that gave Moto Guzzi a run for their money in 1955 and 1956.

It sprang from a 125 cc single and 250 cc twin. The single, with a cylindrical inlet valve across the back of the crankcase, went well enough. But when it was doubled-up into a 250 cc parallel twin, the lengthened valve, fed by a carburettor at one end only, gave different-length inlet tracts for the two crankcases – a hopeless arrangement. The solution was to reposition the valve fore and aft between the two crankcases, with the carb at the rear and the magneto at the front.

Improvement though that was, DKW had become disenchanted with the cylindrical valve, with its gear drive, overlong tract and relatively slow port opening. So they simply switched to piston-controlled induction, put a third cylinder in place of the valve and slightly reduced the bore and stroke to bring the total capacity below 350 cc. Hence the peculiar cylinder layout – one horizontal, the others sloping. August Hobl took second and third places in the world championship in 1955 and 1956 respectively but the factory then pulled out.

The most persistent problem in two-stroke development has been to give the engine reliability and stamina. The trouble stems from distortion of the cylinder (which is hot on the exhaust side, cool on the transfer side) and scanty lubrication (a generous oil supply for the connecting-rod bearings causes plug-fouling).

When the 50 cc championship was introduced in 1962 and Degner's air-cooled Suzuki single showed such unexpected dependability, the answer was clear – small cylinders distorted less, their pistons ran cooler and their big ends were not so highly stressed. Twice later the lesson was emphasised – first, when Suzuki gave the tiny engine two cylinders, which not only raised its power (through higher peak revs) but also enhanced its stamina; second, when they changed to water cooling (with an impeller), which tended to equalise temperatures around the cylinder port belt.

Early on, the Japanese, notably Yamaha and Suzuki, used a double lubrication system – the usual small proportion of oil in the petrol, plus a tiny pumped feed to various bearings. Nowadays, however, most grand-prix engines have abandoned the pump, which, linked to the twistgrip to vary the delivery, is confined to roadsters – to reduce the supply at small throttle openings rather than increase it for full power.

In the 1960s, the benefits of small cylinders and water cooling spread quickly up the capacity scale, where Yamaha were most successful. After perfecting a 125 cc disc-valve parallel twin, they doubled it up into a 250 cc V-four, then scaled that down to 125 cc, and Phil Read won both titles in 1968.

Walter Kaaden, at MZ, was not the only engineer who could not afford such refinements. Dr Eduardo Giro, at Ossa in Spain, had to exercise his talents on an air-cooled single in the 250 cc class, and a phenomenal job he made of it, taking his lone rider, Santiago Herrero, to third place in the 1969 championship.

Giro naturally chose a disc inlet valve, with the largest carburettor he could find (42 mm). The 70×65 mm cylinder had enormous ports and squish area, and deep finning to stiffen the walls. A welded aluminium monocoque frame-cum-fuel tank helped keep weight down to 220 lb.

The engine's tractability was outstanding, with useful power from 6,500 rpm to the amazing safe limit of 11,500 (peak power, 42 bhp, was at 10,000 to 11,000). Top speed was about 140 mph and fuel consumption an admirable 30 mpg. A remarkable achievement.

The FIM's restriction on cylinder numbers, mentioned in the second paragraph of this chapter, caused a hiccough in the upward trend in engine power, hence race speeds, at the end of the 1960s. At the same time, gear ratios were limited to six, which put an end to 50 cc power bands no wider than a few hundred rpm with up to 18 gears (Kreidler) or 14 (Suzuki) to compensate.

As a result, in that and the 125 cc classes, competition became increasingly a matter of port design, with West German Jorg Möller proving especially successful, producing championship-winning engines for Kreidler, Morbidelli and Minarelli.

Restricted to two cylinders, the 250 cc Yamaha (and Aermacchi and Harley-Davidson), with their rear-facing carburettors, had an aerodynamic advantage over the disc-valvers so long as the cylinders were mounted abreast – their side-facing carburettors made the disc-valve engines (hence the dolphin fairings) much wider. The solution, again pioneered by MZ, was to mount the cylinders in tandem – an arrangement later adopted by Kawasaki on Kork Ballington's and Toni Mang's highly successful 250 and 350 cc twins.

In the 500 class, where four cylinders are allowed, there is little to choose in width between the two types of engine. Yamaha virtually couple two parallel twins side by side for a transverse four-in-line, while Suzuki and Kawasaki both arrive at a square-four layout, though by different routes. Since Suzuki's disc-valve twins were always side by side, the RG500, like their unsuccessful 250 cc square four in 1964, can be regarded as a twin with two more cylinders grafted on the front, whereas Kawasaki's KR500 is virtually a tandem twin with another two cylinders on the right.

Another notable difference is that Yamaha, again for commercial reasons, use monoshock rear springing, with a long suspension strut above the engine, while Kawasaki and Suzuki connect the rear fork to an upright strut via a rocker arm, with the geometry designed to increase the effective spring rate as the wheel moves upward.

The sidecar championship (500 cc) was the last to fall to the two-stroke. For the first five years it was dominated by Norton singles with bolt-on chassis – four titles going to Eric Oliver and one to Cyril Smith, in the face of stiff opposition from Gilera fours. It was Oliver who pioneered the kneeler chassis

75

(to reduce frontal area and lower the centre of gravity) and extensive streamlining to cut down air drag.

By 1954, however, the BMW flat twin, with pivoted front fork, had asserted its all-round superiority, which it reinforced with a phenomenal string of 19 individual and 19 manufacturers' titles. It had everything going for it – the flat engine permitted an ultra-low centre of gravity for easy drifting without risk of rolling over; the engine was torquey and smooth, with the jutting cylinders well placed for cooling; and the shaft transmission was robust and practically trouble-free.

Only twice was it beaten by a four-stroke. That was Helmut Fath's home-built four-abreast Urs – with an equally low centre of gravity and a decisive power surplus. Fath, who first showed his engineering talents by winning the 1960 championship on a home-tuned BMW, scorned orthodoxy. His Urs engine had the crankpins spaced at 90 degrees, instead of the usual 180, and each inlet valve was fed by two ports, one of them injected.

Driving the outfit himself, he regained the title in 1968. Three years later, Horst Owesle, with a further 10 bhp from Keihin carburettors, high-lift cams and revised oiling, drove the Urs to its second championship.

Inevitably, however, the two-stroke's extra power and lighter weight proved decisive, first (in 1975 and 1976) through Konig flat-four outboard engines, then through Yamaha straight fours. After that, progress switched to chassis and suspension design, with hub-centre steering and side-car-wheel steering both aimed at higher cornering speeds and fewer acrobatics from the passenger.

This trend culminated in Rolf Biland's two-wheel-drive Beo, in which the passenger was no more than human ballast. After the Beo took the title in 1978, the FIM banned progressive design, then backtracked by running two separate championships in 1979, one for traditional outfits, the other for advanced layouts. Finally, for 1980, they reverted to a single formula allowing advanced suspension at the rear but not at the front – a sure recipe for understeer. But Biland's LCR beat the rules with an ingenious slotted steering layout.

SIX

Racing in a New Decade – the 1970s

In many ways the 1970s moved off to a predictable start. My old adversary Agostini looked like going on for ever in the 500 cc class and, with little major opposition in that first year, took the title once more by a large margin, winning all ten races in which he competed. Having secured the title, there was little point in his competing in the final grand prix in Spain, which was won by Bergamonti, also on an MV Agusta machine. The season's best challenge came somewhat surprisingly from New Zealand's Ginger Molloy on one of the new three-cylinder Kawasaki HIR machines. This was the first indication of a two-stroke invasion of the 500 cc class, for until the 1970s the class had been dominated by four-stroke machinery. Molloy finished second in France, Finland, Northern Ireland and Spain. It was a similar story in the 350 cc class. Ago swept through the racing calendar, winning the nine rounds out of the ten he felt obliged to contest.

The FIM introduced more restrictions, limiting 125 cc and 250 cc machines to twin-cylinders and six-speed gearboxes. In this way they hoped to encourage some of the smaller manufacturers back. Derbi, Kreidler and the small Jamathi factory from Holland were by now competing with 50 cc machines, but Angel Nieto, despite his impetuous style of riding, which exposed him too often to falling, collected his second world title in two years for the Derbi factory. The talented Spanish rider did equally well in the 125 cc class, but Dieter Braun, riding a Suzuki, did better and had clinched the title by mid-season. Yamaha dominated the 250 cc class, Britain's Rodney Gould taking the title from Australia's Kel Carruthers and Sweden's Kent Andersson.

Significant to world-championship racing in 1971 was the return of Phil Read, which was to have far-reaching effects.

Phil had preferred to ride in British races, with only the occasional continental outing, but in 1971 he rode a specially prepared Yamaha which incorporated a new frame of his own design. It was enough to give him the 250 cc title after a close-fought battle with Rodney Gould and Jarno Saarinen. Racing was also keen in the lower classes. In the final round of the 50 cc championship, Nieto fell and Jan de Vries raced on to win the race and the title by just six points. Significant too, in 1971, was the performance in the 125 cc class of Barry Sheene, on an ex-works Suzuki he had bought from Stuart Graham. Barry led the championship table with just the final round to be raced in Spain. But this time luck was with Nieto and as Barry's machine began to slow down, he made certain of the title as he crossed the line first.

In the heavier classes Agostini continued to have things all his own way, but there were signs in the 350 cc class that things were beginning to happen which might upset the rock-hard supremacy of Agostini and MV. Phil Read rode second to Ago in Holland, and the new sensation from Finland, Jarno Saarinen, won in Czechoslovakia and Italy and was second to Agostini in Finland. The signs were not misplaced, for Saarinen started 1972 in brilliant style. Riding a new water-cooled Yamaha, he beat Agostini in the opening round in Germany and proved his victory was no fluke by winning again in France, where Agostini finished down in fourth place. Count Agusta acted quickly by providing Ago with a new four-cylinder 350 machine and by signing Phil Read to support the Italian. In the end it was close, but Agostini retained the title with 102 points against Saarinen's 89. In the 500 cc class, Pagani supported Agostini on MV and they comfortably held off the opposition. Angel Nieto proved his supremacy on lightweight machinery, winning both the 50 cc and 125 cc world titles.

As the 1973 season approached, it was possible to detect a shift of emphasis in grand-prix racing. Yamaha, who were already well represented in 125 cc and 250 cc racing – and to some extent in the 350 cc class – were now set to challenge MV Agusta with powerful 500 cc machinery. With new models and the volatile riding of Saarinen, it was more than just a show of bravery. Count Agusta took the threat seriously and signed Phil Read to ride with Agostini in a determined effort to keep the world crown. The stage was set and for the first time in years there was the prospect of some exciting racing in the 500 cc class. Dramatically, the first round at the Paul Ricard circuit in France went to Yamaha. Saarinen, fastest in practice, was soon out in front in the race, challenged strongly by Agostini. The new Yamahas were very fast and Saarinen rode fearlessly to keep in front. In an effort to stay in touch Agostini came off, leaving Saarinen to take maximum points. Phil Read nudged ahead of Saarinen's co-rider in the Yamaha team, Hideo Kanaya, to take second place.

In the second round in Austria, Yamaha did even better. MV took their biggest-ever battering, wilting under the Yamaha challenge. Agostini and Read failed to finish (in the 350 cc race as well as the 500) as Yamaha made factory history by winning all the four solo classes at the meeting. The 500 cc race was won by Saarinen at an average of 104.67 mph, with a fastest lap of 106.75 mph, and Kanaya finished in second position. For the first time in years, it was now evident that MV had some real opposition and a disconsolate Agostini travelled to the third round in West Germany without a point to his name. Events at the Hockenheim circuit did nothing to improve his state of mind, for he was forced to retire with engine trouble when only four laps from home. But the race was really between Read and Saarinen. Phil seemed determined to show the Finn who was boss and, despite repeated efforts by Saarinen to get in front, Read was able to bring MV their first grand-prix victory of the season. Altogether, though, it was a disastrous meeting for the Italian factory. They were totally routed in the 350 cc class where, after Agostini had set a new class lap record at 104.4 mph (later to retire), Lansivuori raced ahead to win and put himself 35 points ahead of Ago in the championship table.

Yamaha were also doing incredibly well in the 125 cc and 250 cc championships. Kent Andersson had won all three races so far held in the series, and the devastating Jarno Saarinen had done likewise in the 250 cc events. As the riders travelled to Italy for the fourth round, Yamaha were well ahead in four of the five solo classes, the only exception being the 50 cc class which they were not contesting.

The disaster at Monza – the worst in the history of world-championship racing – changed all that. Only 800 yards from the start of the 250 cc event, a horrific, fifteen-machine, 120 mph pile-up claimed the lives of Jarno Saarinen and Renzo Pasolini, the 350 cc Italian champion, who had been riding for Harley-Davidson. The race was abandoned and the 500 cc and sidecar events cancelled. The tragedy changed the entire course of grand-prix racing in 1973, for Yamaha announced that as a mark of respect they would not officially contest any further grands prix that year, and flew their 500 cc machines back to Japan for further development. This left the way clear for MV, but Agostini's problems were never re-solved. Read saw his chance to press home his advantage, winning in Holland, Sweden and Spain to take the 500 cc world title from the Italian who had won it for the last seven years. Ago recovered well in the second half of the season, but his wins in Belgium, Czechoslovakia and Finland were not enough to make up for his disastrous early round perform-ances and he dropped to third place in the championship positions. He did, however, enjoy the consolation of retain-ing the 350 cc crown, wins in Holland and Finland being just enough to put him ahead of Lansivuori at the end of the season. Yamaha dominated the 125 cc and 250 cc events, Kent Andersson taking the former title and Dieter Braun the latter. In the 50 cc class, Jan de Vries regained the title from Nieto, who had switched to Morbidelli after Derbi pulled out of racing, riding the Kreidler.

The sensation of 1974 was Agostini's move to Yamaha. To put it mildly, he was unhappy at the way Phil Read supposedly worked himself into Count Agusta's favour, but where results were all-important, it was no real surprise that MV were beginning to look upon Read as their number one rider. Ago was outspoken in his criticism of Read and there had been rumours that he was angling for a works ride with Honda, who were reputedly going to return to racing. But at a specially called press conference in December 1973,

Agostini and Rodney Gould, Yamaha's European executive, announced a two-year contract for the Italian with the Japanese factory. Another reason for Ago's move was his desire to compete in the 750 cc class. Yamaha could offer him these rides, MV could not. Read signed for MV Agusta, who also brought in Gianfranco Bonera in support. The 500 cc championship looked to be hotting up considerably as Suzuki, through their British subsidiary, moved into 500 cc racing with a team comprising Barry Sheene, Paul Smart and Jack Findlay.

Within two seasons the 500 cc championship had been turned upside-down, as three highly competitive factories – MV Agusta, Yamaha and Suzuki – lined up for the season's opening encounter in France. After Sheene had moved into an early lead, Agostini took the Yamaha ahead and held on for three laps, before his engine gave out, letting Read through to give the first success to MV. Not for many years had the 500 cc class seen such drama and interest. In Germany the top riders refused to appear because they considered the Nurburgring too dangerous. In Austria Agostini rode the Yamaha to victory after Read's MV had seized. In Italy it looked like Ago's race again, after a brilliant dice with Sheene and the MV-mounted Bonera, but the Yamaha ran dry of fuel with just a lap to go and Bonera roared ahead to win. In Holland Ago won decisively, breaking the lap record to become the first rider to lap the van Drenthe circuit in under three minutes, but in Belgium Read showed he was still in the chase, leading from beginning to end and setting a new lap record at 133.4 mph, the fastest lap ever recorded to that time in a world-championship round. Read's win was in spite of Yamaha's new lighter machine, which had been flown in specially for the race. Agostini lost the advantage when he unfortunately crashed after Sheene's Suzuki seized ahead of him. His damaged shoulder put paid to his challenge in the remaining rounds and Phil Read collected his second 500 cc world title for the second time in two years.

But Agostini in some measure had his revenge on MV, for he won the 350 cc title for Yamaha after winning it for MV for the previous six years. Incidentally, Phil Read's success in

1973 was the first by a British rider in the 500 cc class since my own success, on the MV, in 1965. Kent Andersson was good enough to bring Yamaha their second successive title in the 125 cc class, but their efforts were thwarted in 250 cc racing, Walter Villa on a Harley-Davidson taking the title from Dieter Braun. Following Pasolini's fatal crash on the Harley-Davidson in the Monza pile-up the year before, the American factory had withdrawn from racing, but had signed Walter Villa and Michel Rougerie for 1974. In the 50 cc class, Henk Van Kessel, riding the Van Veen Kreidler on which the now-retired Jan de Vries had taken the title in 1973, had a comparatively easy passage to win the championship in 1974.

Sheene's heavily publicised crash at Daytona spoilt the early-season prospects, but in 1975 only one champion was destined to retain his title. That was Walter Villa, who won 250 cc races in Germany, Spain, Italy, Holland and Sweden to put him ahead of team mate Rougerie, who took second place, and Braun on the Yamaha, who finished third. In the 50 cc class, Angel Nieto was back with a vengeance after a dismal interlude in 125 cc racing the previous year. On the Van Veen Kreidler, the Spaniard won six of the eight classic races to give him the title from Lazzarini on a Piovaticci and van Zeebroeck on a Kreidler. In the 125 cc class, brilliant work by Jorg Möller, who had previously produced the Van Veen Kreidler racers at the tiny Morbidelli factory in Italy, was amply rewarded. The new water-cooled two-strokes ridden by Paolo Pileri and Pierpaolo Bianchi ousted the Yamahas to finish first and second in the championship.

The new name in 350 cc racing in 1975 was undoubtedly Johnny Cecotto from Venezuela. This pop-style teenager from Caracas became the youngest-ever world champion with wins in France, Italy, Germany and Finland. His major challenge came from Agostini, riding one of the official factory Yamahas new that season, but as Ago began to set his sights more clearly on the 500 cc crown later in the season, Cecotto looked a good bet for honours at his first real attempt. Financed by the Yamaha importers in Venezuela, he rode the non-works Yamaha to his first world championship, clinching the title with his victory in Finland.

In the 500 cc class, competition had not been so keen for many years. Suzuki, Harley-Davidson, Yamaha, and MV Agusta, of course, and even Kawasaki, thought it worthwhile getting into the act and the amount of rider talent on show was staggering: Agostini and Kanaya for Yamaha, Sheene and Lansivuori for Suzuki, Read and Armando Toracca, the Italian 250 cc champion drafted in for the injured Bonera, for MV, and Mick Grant and the fearless French-Canadian rider Yvon Duhamel for Kawasaki. The Harley-Davidson challenge did not materialise because their new machine proved uncompetitive, and Kawasaki made little impression, but the remainder produced some fine racing and a sparkling season.

Agostini was desperate to win back the title which he felt rightfully belonged to him and not Read, and he gained confidence with a win in the opening round in France. Kanaya finished second and Read third. History was recorded in Austria when Kanaya became the first Japanese rider to win a 500 cc world-championship race. It was here that Sheene, recovered from his Daytona crash but not fully mobile, was forbidden to allow someone to push-start him and was ordered off the line, even though the organisers had allowed him to practise and qualify for the race. The German round produced a thrilling race, hotly contested by Read and Agostini. Agostini eventually crossed the line first, as he did again in Italy, inspired and dominant before his home crowd. With the recognised stars boycotting the Isle of Man round, Mick Grant took the HIRA Kawasaki to its first and only success in a world-championship round. Sheene took Suzuki to the front ahead of Agostini, in the last seconds, to win the round in Holland, but Read, generally comfortably at home in Belgium, won on the fast Spa-Francorchamps circuit, establishing a new record average speed. Sheene, however, almost snatched victory with a new record lap at 135.75 mph. At this point Read was a few points ahead of Agostini in the championship race and the Italian's chances weren't improved by a retirement in the Swedish round. In Finland Read had the chance of retaining the title, but just when it seemed the race was his, his machine broke down. Bonera crashed and Agostini luckily raced on to win. He was now ahead of

Read on points and the situation was tense as the riders travelled to Czechoslovakia. The odds were with Agostini, for he only had to finish in the first six to win the title. Read won – but Ago was the second rider home and thus regained the title.

In a way, it was the end of an era, for the veterans Giacomo Agostini and Phil Read were now virtually at the end of the road and a new breed of racers were ready to take over. The second half of the 1970s belongs to Barry Sheene, American riders like Roberts, Baker, Hennen, and new names in the grand-prix circuits like Gregg Hansford, Kork Ballington and Italy's Virginio Ferrari.

Yamaha's decision not to have an official works team in 1976 gave Suzuki the chance to move in. Agostini formed his own team and he was provided with bikes by MV Agusta, who were by now unimpressed with Phil Read's performances. Sheene moved off to a magnificent start, winning in France, despite the handicap of a leg broken in an accident at Cadwell Park at the end of the previous season. After some close and exciting racing involving eight or nine riders, Sheene eventually emerged to win the second round in Austria. Agostini on the MV had been totally outpaced in the two early rounds and for the Italian round he raced one of the RG500 cc Suzuki racers, which were replicas of the factory machines of 1975, a batch of which had been marketed for 1976. Ago set the pace and the fastest lap, but after he retired with a seized engine on the fourteenth lap, Sheene and Read treated the crowd to a fine display of riding, Sheene emerging as the winner to give him three victories in a row.

Sheene won yet again in Holland and although he was beaten by team mate John Williams in Belgium, a further win in Sweden gave him the title. Agostini reverted to MV for the German Grand Prix and won this final round, Read by this time having announced his retirement from world-championship racing. Angel Nieto and Walter Villa retained their titles in the 50 cc and 250 cc classes respectively. Villa had a particularly good season by beating Cecotto to the 350 cc crown. In the 125 cc class Bianchi won his first world title on the Morbidelli. During the close season Nieto had switched to Bultaco, and it was on this machine that he took the title from Lazzarini on the Kreidler.

After a year in which they were totally absent from the world-championship tables, Yamaha returned to the 500 cc class in 1977 with Steve Baker and Johnny Cecotto as their team riders. Agostini, reluctant even to fade away, was given a works Yamaha for his own team, sponsored by Marlboro. Joining Barry Sheene in the Suzuki line-up were American Pat Hennen and British rider Steve Parrish. To get the season off to a flying start, Yamaha introduced new 500 cc machines, but at the opening event in San Carlos, Venezuela, it was Sheene who opened the scoring with a fine win for Suzuki. Cecotto's challenge ended in Austria, where he crashed and broke an arm in the 350 cc race. Because of the lack of organisation at the track many of the 500 cc riders refused to race. Sheene rode the Suzuki to another win in Germany, and yet another in Italy, setting new lap records at both circuits. After Baker looked like taking the Yamaha to victory in France, he was sprayed with fuel when his filler cap opened and, while he was clearing his vision, Sheene seized his chance and moved ahead to win yet again. Although Barry was beaten by Wil Hartog in the Dutch event, he clinched the 500 cc title for the second year running with wins in Belgium, Sweden and Finland. Steve Baker finished in second position and Pat Hennen was third at the end of the season. Nieto on the Bultaco repeated his success of 1976 to take the 1977 50 cc title and Bianchi on the Morbidelli did the same in the 125 cc class. The 250 cc Harley-Davidsons of Villa and Uncini were eclipsed by Mario Lega on the Morbidelli, who took the title for the first time. Katayama became Japan's first-ever world champion, winning the 350 cc title on a Dutch-built Yamaha.

From then until the end of the decade, the American Kenny Roberts was supreme in the premier class of motor-cycle racing, the 500s. He outrode Barry Sheene and Johnny Cecotto in 1978, and Virginio Ferrari and Barry again in 1979. His performances were convincing, although in 1978 only ten points separated him from Sheene at the end of the day. Roberts was determined to keep his title in 1979, but he had a disastrous start, crashing while testing a new Yamaha in

85

Japan. His injured back kept him out of the first round in Venezuela and Sheene won the race from Ferrari and Tom Herron. Roberts won in Austria, with Sheene unplaced, but in Germany the American was pushed into second place by the Dutchman Wil Hartog, riding a Suzuki. Sheene had machine problems there and was in trouble again in Italy, while Roberts raced through to win. As the season progressed, Barry dropped further behind, mainly through machine problems and bad luck, while Kenny's position strengthened. Further wins put him ahead of Ferrari. In Belgium the top riders refused to ride because of the state of the track, and in Sweden Sheene beat Roberts comprehensively. But when Ferrari crashed in the French Grand Prix, Roberts was sure of the title.

In 50 cc racing, Ricardo Tormo of Spain on a Bultaco took the title in 1978 and Eugenio Lazzarini of Italy on a Van Veen Kreidler in 1979. Lazzarini (on an MBA) and Nieto (on a Minarelli) were 125 cc world champions in 1978 and 1979, but the other major news, along with the emergence of Kenny Roberts as a new and outstanding rider of the classic rounds, was the remarkable success of Kawasaki and Kork Ballington. Kork, who had been racing for quite some time with little distinction in the grands prix, so dominated both series that he was 250 cc and 350 cc double world champion both years, giving Kawasaki their first real breakthrough in championship racing. Gregg Hansford, also riding Kawasaki, was runner-up in the 250 cc class both years.

Barry – The Modern Idol

The only new British rider to make a name for himself in grand-prix racing in the 1970s and early 1980s is Barry Sheene. Alone, the success and personality of this international superstar has kept Britain in touch with world-championship racing. The record books tell the sad story, for without Barry the last British world champion in any class would have been Phil Read – way back in 1974.

Sheene took the title in 1976 and 1977. Encouraged by his

father, Frank Sheene, a well-known rider, Barry made his racing debut in 1968. Two years later he was 125 cc British champion. His first grand-prix victory was in Belgium in 1971 on his first visit to the fast Spa-Francorchamps circuit and that same year he almost took the 125 cc world title. With further wins in Sweden and Finland, the championship was decided in the final round in Spain. Angel Nieto won, to take the title by just eight points.

A disappointing spell with Yamaha in 1972 ended when Sheene signed for the Suzuki GB team for 1973. He had now moved up to heavier machinery and became the FIM Formula 750 cc champion that year as well as dominating racing on British circuits. Britain was desperately in need of a new hero and Barry filled the bill admirably. He was outspoken without giving offence, likeable and easy to get on with, honest in expressing his views, and he had that relaxed, informal way which came over well with the media. Above all, he was riding superbly and after racing works Suzukis in 1974 he finished sixth in the 500 cc world championship. That year he won the first British Grand Prix at Silverstone, taking four-fifths of a second off the lap record and averaging 106.22 mph for the first 20 laps, making this the fastest motor-cycle race ever held at Silverstone to that time.

Barry looked a good bet for his first world championship in 1975, but a dramatic crash at Daytona, from which he was fortunate to escape with his life, ended that possibility. It also thrust him into the headlines all round the world. There were further crashes that year, but his luck changed in 1976. He faced tough opposition from riders like Johnny Cecotto, Marco Lucchinelli, Phil Read and Tepi Lansivuori, but in the end he gained his first world championship with comparative ease on the Suzuki RG500 four. He secured the title in Sweden in the eighth round and, never slow to exploit the commercial value of his success, said he would not ride in the remaining rounds unless he was offered better start money. He wasn't – and so did not ride in another grand-prix race that year.

By 1976 the Americans were interested in world-championship racing, particularly the new Formula 750 cc

Championship with Steve Baker, Kenny Roberts, Gene Romero and Mike Baldwin joining in, but in the 500 cc championship, Barry's toughest opposition came from Steve Baker on a Yamaha and Pat Hennen on a Suzuki. In the end Sheene took the title for the second year running in easy style, and by now was recognised as the most exciting and colourful motor-cycle racer around.

He looked set to make it three in a row, but the American Kenny Roberts had other ideas and Barry forfeited the title, being ten points behind Roberts at the end of the season. He was even less consistent in the first half of the new season and although he recovered well in the second half, he finished third in 1979 behind Roberts, and Virginio Ferrari of Italy on a Suzuki.

A switch back to Yamaha in 1980 proved disastrous and as Roberts went on to take the title yet again, Barry finished way down in equal fourteenth position. Despite his lack of success he remained popular, and in 1981 he again rode Yamaha to finish the season in fourth place in the 500 cc class.

For the traditionalists, Barry Sheene may well appear brash and arrogant, too commercially motivated and ready to speak his mind. His criticism of the TT Course and his refusal to ride on the Island lost him friends, but above all else Barry is his own man and is not afraid to stand by his convictions. His fan following is enormous, not only in Britain, and at the end of 1981 he showed he was still capable of grabbing headlines. He was said to have been offered almost £250,000 by former multi-World Champion Giacomo Agostini to ride in his Marlboro-sponsored Yamaha team for 1982. But even then Barry wasn't sure, because he had up his sleeve what he considered to be another massive sponsorship deal which would allow him to run his own team.

Formula 750

For all its promise, Formula 750 cc racing didn't last long as a world-championship series. Granted full status in 1977, when American racer Steve Baker took the title, it lasted only two more seasons at top level. Baker totally dominated that first, exciting season. Of the eleven events, he won five (at Daytona, Jarama, Brands Hatch, Salzburgring and Zolder), and finished in second place three times (at Imola, Assen and Laguna Seca). He ended the season with a magnificent 131 points. The French rider Christian Sarron was next best with 55 points.

There is no doubt that in the factory Yamaha OW31, Steve had the best bike, but his performance was staggering just the same. It was his first full season of racing in Europe and the frail-looking, bespectacled 25-year-old from Washington State was quick to show his talent. Despite his success he lost Yamaha's favour at the end of the season and returned to contest the series in 1978 as a privateer, riding a 750 cc Yamaha for the Venezuelan importers.

But 1978 was Johnny Cecotto's year. The Venezuelan whizz-kid who had staggered Daytona when only nineteen by finishing third after starting from the back of the second row of the grid, was at twenty-three a national hero. Riding the official Yamaha entry, he kept Kenny Roberts on a works-prepared but independently tuned Yamaha at bay, to beat him by just five points. Highly talented, Cecotto's Achilles' heel has always been inconsistency, but in 1978 he started well with wins at Imola in Italy and the Paul Ricard circuit in France, and did enough in the remaining rounds to fend off Roberts's insistent challenge. In the end he won three of the ten rounds. Roberts won four rounds, but Cecotto's impressive list of three second places and one third was just enough to keep him in front.

On this form Kenny Roberts looked a certain winner for the 1979 season, but he decided instead to go for the 500 cc world title, which he took for the second year running. His lack of success in Formula 750 cc racing enabled Patrick Pons to take the title and become France's first-ever motor-cycling world champion.

Cecotto set off strongly to defend his title. His third and second places in the two legs of the opening round in Italy put him ahead and he consolidated his position in the second round at Brands Hatch by winning both races. It was in

France that Pons got into his stride, winning the first heat and finishing second in the following race. Good performances in Austria, Canada and, particularly, West Germany, where he won both races, were enough to give him the last 750 cc world title by 154 points to Michel Frutschi's 132.

It was the growing popularity of the high-powered super-bikes and the increasing inclination of American racers to compete in Europe that underlined the importance of Formula 750 cc racing. The class was given international status in 1973, but soon ran into problems, some organisers even going so far as to cancel their scheduled 750 cc championship races. Barry Sheene took the first Formula 750 prize on a Suzuki in 1973, but thereafter the championship was monopolised by Yamaha entries. Australians John Dodds and Jack Findlay were the new champions in 1974 and 1975, and in 1976 Victor Palomo of Spain was declared the winner, after a drama in the second round at San Carlos in Venezuela brought chaos and confusion to the championship. There was a total mix-up in the results. Gary Nixon was first declared the overall winner of the two races. This decision was withdrawn and Steve Baker was then declared champion. Nixon protested, but the issue wasn't settled until after the end of the season, when at first we had the ludicrous situation of both Victor Palomo and Gary Nixon claiming themselves champions. Not until October, at a special meeting, did the FIM delete the Venezuelan results, a decision which made Palomo the champion.

The 750 cc world championship set out with high hopes of becoming the ultimate class – a kind of Formula 1 of motor-cycle racing – but this never materialised. Although it seemed a good idea at the time, poorly chosen dates for some of the rounds, improbable venues where support was marginal, and the way the rules allowed Yamaha machines to fill the entries, made Formula 750 cc racing as a world championship tame and uninteresting, and finally killed it off.

SEVEN

Three Wheels Instead of Two

Sidecars are not 'commercial' in the modern world, yet sidecar racing is spectacular and gives an added dimension to any race programme. That is why a sidecar class had been included in the world championships from the start in 1949. When ordinary people used to buy motor-cycle combinations as they do solo machines today, historic names like Bert Le Vack, Charlie Collier, Freddie Barnes, Harry Langman, Freddie Dixon, Graham Walker and George Tucker dominated sidecar racing. By 1949 and the start of the new world championships, Eric Oliver was the big name. He put Britain firmly ahead by winning that first-ever sidecar world championship on his British-built Norton combination. Oliver and Norton, despite considerable opposition from the Italian Gilera factory, with passengers Denis Jenkinson, Lorenzo Dobelli and Stanley Dibben, set the standard in those early post-war years, Oliver gaining the title in 1949, 1950, 1951 and 1953. In 1952 Oliver broke a leg in a racing accident and this allowed Cyril Smith to move in to take the title for Britain.

The tide turned against Britain in 1954 when Oliver on his (by now) famous Norton/Watsonian outfit faced a strong challenge from Wilhelm Noll riding a BMW. Oliver won the first three rounds, on the Isle of Man, in Northern Ireland and Belgium, and looked set to take the title yet again, but he broke an arm in a non-championship race. Noll and Fritz Cron, with the factory-backed BMW, seized their chance and took the title to start the famous German factory's astonishing long-term domination of the class.

From 1954, right through to 1967, BMW-powered sidecar outfits won the world championship – fourteen years without interruption. The German engine's low-speed torque and remarkable reliability made it ideal for sidecar racing and it stayed well ahead of all opposition. For eight years BMW machines occupied the five top positions in the sidecar world championships. Along with the domination of sidecar racing by the German BMW was the almost total authority of German riders in the class. Through Wilhelm Noll, Wilhelm Faust, Fritz Hillebrand, Walter Schneider, Helmut Fath and then the remarkable Max Deubel, who won four titles in a row, German riders took the championship from 1954 to 1964. It was the tall and talented Swiss rider Fritz Scheidegger who robbed Deubel of the title in 1965. With wins in Germany, Holland, Belgium and Italy, he and his British passenger, John Robinson, finished just six points ahead of the German sidecar ace. After winning the title again in 1966, Scheidegger and Robinson were going for their third title in a row, but a crash at Mallory Park in an early season meeting ended in tragedy. Robinson was badly hurt and the well-liked Swiss rider was killed.

The West German Klaus Enders was supreme in 1967, but Helmut Fath, a year later, caused a sensation by winning the championship on his own machine, the Urs. Fath had been world champion in 1960, but injuries sustained the following year kept him out of racing. When he was ready to return, he had difficulty in getting an engine out of the BMW factory, so he designed and built his own, taking the name from his home town Ursenbach. The four-cylinder, fuel-injected engine was fast and reliable, and it gave Fath the world championship in 1968. He finished in second place with the same machine in 1969 and Horst Owesle rode it to take the championship yet again in 1971.

By this time, however, Klaus Enders was the top man in international sidecar racing. After Fath's surprising success in 1968, Enders was world champion in 1969, 1970, 1972, 1973 and 1974. By then, the long run of BMW successes was at an end and Rolf Steinhausen kept the West German rider tradition alive for just two more years, the Swiss rider Rolf Biland then taking over. But in 1977 Britain took the sidecar world championship for the first time since Eric Oliver's last victory in 1953, when George O'Dell and his Yamaha/Windle outfit were supreme. O'Dell, remarkably, did not win a single grand prix all season, but his consistently good form and high placings put him ahead of the field at the end of the year.

In 1978 Rolf Biland caused a storm with his remarkable Beo/Yamaha outfit, which, though contravening no rules, was so revolutionary and so far in advance of all traditional sidecar outfits, that the authorities felt obliged to put it, and similar outfits, in a class of their own in 1979. Biland took the B2A title and Bruno Holzer, also of Switzerland, won the B2B championship. It was all too complicated and the FIM reverted to just one championship for 1980 as Britain claimed her seventh sidecar world title through Jock Taylor and his Swedish passenger Benga Johansson, on the Yamaha outfit. But the remarkable Biland was back in 1981 to gain his third world title in four years.

Many sidecar racers who didn't win world titles have contributed substantially to the championships. During the long domination by Germany, British interests were kept alive through Chris Vincent, Pip Harris and Colin Seeley. Vincent's victory in the sidecar TT in 1962 was the first there by a British rider for eight years, and ten years later he and passenger Mike Casey finished fourth in the world championship. Pip Harris claimed third place in the championship in 1960 and Colin Seeley was third in 1964 and again in 1966.

The West German rider Heinz Luthringhauser lost his left leg in a car accident in 1961, but had the controls switched over so that he could continue racing. He was placed second in the championship in 1972, despite an accident in the Czechoslovakian Grand Prix that year in which his passenger, Hans Jurgen Cusnik, was killed. In terms of sidecar design Florian Camathias made a major contribution. This respected Swiss rider developed a sidecar which was very low to the ground, and which became the basic prototype for the modern outfits that followed. He was second in the world championships of 1962 and 1963 on his BMW-powered outfits.

The most successful world-championship sidecar racer is Klaus Enders, with five championships in six years. This remarkable West German rider retired in 1974 after a disagreement with his sponsor, Gerhardt Heukerot, and Dieter

Busch who built his outfits and tuned the special BMW engines he used.

Over the years the design of sidecars and the techniques of riding them have changed significantly. The early models were open chargers, and more like ancient chariots as seen against the sleek, sophisticated units of today. Riders gave up sitting on their machines in the traditional way long ago, and now kneel in position. Their courage and skills are still as necessary as speeds have increased, and whatever the commercial value of sidecars, there are few who would deny their value in a race programme.

How the Circuits have Changed

Grand-prix circuits, like racing riders and racing factories, come and go. Some which were used at the start, like Spa in Belgium, are still famous racing circuits. Others, like Berne in Switzerland, have gone for good. Some I raced on were so unbelievably bad in terms of safety precautions and facilities, that you wondered how on earth they had ever been chosen in the first place. One of the most enduring is at Assen where the Dutch TT has been held for more than thirty years. It is a popular circuit, well maintained and organised, and draws large and enthusiastic crowds. Improved over the years, it is a credit to the sport and is likely to go on for ever as a grand-prix circuit.

Yet nothing is certain. In the 1950s and 1960s no one could have envisaged the world championships without the famous, historic Mountain Circuit on the Isle of Man. Yet it came to an end as a grand-prix circuit in 1976, killed-off by star riders' criticisms, faster and more sophisticated motor cycles, and an increasingly long list of crashes and fatalities.

To be fair, I think statistics show that the Isle of Man was no more dangerous in terms of miles raced than some other grand-prix circuits which haven't been axed from the programme. But emotionally the odds were against its survival for world-championship racing as opposition generally grew to the use of natural road courses. It was also very long, more than 37 miles round, making it hard for riders to get to know it well. But in the earlier days the anti-TT lobby was as much against the poor cash incentives offered on the Island as against the potential dangers of the course. Agostini eventually came out strongly against it. So did Phil Read, Barry Sheene and others, and they were influential voices. Yet Phil put his principles to one side when Honda offered him a ride there in 1977 in the new Formula 1 event. By a technicality it carried a world-title tag, and Phil boosted his total of championships to eight by winning convincingly. For a long time the authorities fought to keep the Isle of Man TT as a round in the world championships, but the weight of opinion became so strong that there was no real alternative but to transfer the British round to the mainland, and Silverstone was chosen.

The first world championships in 1949 were held at Berne in Switzerland, Assen in Holland, Monza in Italy, the TT course on the Isle of Man, the Dundrod circuit in Northern Ireland and at Spa in Belgium. Thirty years later, with an enlarged grand-prix race programme, the chosen circuits were San Carlos in Venezuela, the Salzburgring in Austria, Hockenheim in West Germany, Imola in Italy, Jarama in Spain, Rijeka (which took over from Opatija) in Yugoslavia, Assen in Holland, Spa-Francorchamps in Belgium, Karlskoga in Sweden, Imatra in Finland, Silverstone in Britain, Brno in Czechoslovakia and Le Mans in France.

At times it has been the custom of the FIM to organise grand-prix races at distant circuits. When the Japanese began to dominate racing, the world-championship calendar for some years included the Suzuka circuit in Japan. Venezuela was another notion, inspired perhaps by the success of its home rider Johnny Cecotto and by the FIM's Andres Ippolito, who promoted the race and was also importer of Yamaha motor cycles into the country. The Argentine also got a grand prix.

The fastest grand-prix circuit is in Belgium at Spa, which had to be changed in the 1970s at the dictate of riders, who were concerned about its safety. The classic Ulster Grand Prix unfortunately lost its world-championship status because of the political troubles in that country, though its long-term future must have been in doubt anyway because it, like the TT circuit, was a natural road course and disfavoured by the new breed of grand-prix riders.

Clermont-Ferrand was the traditional home of the French Grand Prix for many years and was recognised as one of the most picturesque circuits, situated in the mountains of the Auvergne. It was very much a riders' circuit, with plenty of tight bends and numerous gradients. The Brno circuit in Czechoslovakia was first used for a world-championship race in 1965 and although it produced a friendly community feeling, since it wound its way through villages and hollows, it was not favoured by more recent riders because of its natural road characteristics.

Austria was included in the championship round for the first time in 1971, and the specially constructed Salzburgring was used. Situated conveniently close to the German border, it was instantly one of the fastest circuits in Europe. Just over 2½ miles round and relatively simple in layout, the fastest machines could touch 170 mph on the straight sections of the course. But it has not been without its troubles. In 1975 Barry Sheene was ordered off the start line by officials because they considered his earlier crash at Daytona had made him unfit to start without the aid of a 'pusher', and Agostini can only just have escaped disqualification when he defied a 'no slicks' rule at the same meeting. In 1977 there was a multiple crash in the 350 cc race, and riders were horrified at what they saw as the inability of the organisers to deal effectively and speedily with the situation. Riders entered in the following 125 cc race showed their disgust by squatting on the grid and the top 500 cc racers refused to compete.

Opatija in Yugoslavia has also been heavily criticised for its poor safety standards. In 1973 the major factories and riders boycotted the circuit, considering it to be too dangerous, and it was for this reason that the 500 cc race was withdrawn from the circuit the following year. Nonetheless, it brought France her first 350 cc success in world-championship racing for 22 years when Olivier Chevallier, winning his first-ever grand prix, crossed the line first in 1976. The new three-mile, specially constructed circuit at nearby Rijeka took over from Opatija, being used for the first time in 1978.

For sheer drama, the Swedish circuit at Kristianstad in 1961 is still remembered, for it was after the meeting there that the East German rider Ernst Degner defected to the West. While he was there, news came through that the escape from East Germany of his wife and children, which he had been secretly arranging with the help of friends, had been successful, and after the meeting he rushed to Saarbrucken to be reunited with them.

There is a carnival atmosphere at many of the European grands prix, and in Holland the Assen event is one of the country's major sporting occasions. There used to be a similar festival spirit about the East German Grand Prix which for many years was held at Sachsenring. There were side-shows and off-circuit attractions on the eve of the racing and the enormous enthusiasm and the huge crowds of around 200,000 were most impressive. The course was good and interesting, though the road surface could have been better. The history of Sachsenring goes back to before the start of the world-championship series. It was chosen as the venue for the German Grand Prix for the first time in 1934 and two years later the meeting there was designated the Grand Prix of Europe.

A German Grand Prix did not appear in the newly consti-tuted world-championship series until 1952, when it was held at Solitude; and only when the race programme was consider-ably expanded did Sachsenring come back into prominence, staging the East German Grand Prix as a round in the championship for the first time in 1961. I have a particularly soft spot for the circuit because I was the only rider to win three world-championship events there in the same year. That was in 1963 when I won the 250cc, 350 cc and 500 cc races. To celebrate the occasion, the East Germans issued a set of commemorative postage stamps.

Economic factors led to its downfall as a world-championship venue. After 1972 the East German authorities did not apply to be included in the championships and the 'East German' as a separate round ceased to exist. The circuit had its share of tragedies and it was there that Bill Ivy was killed in practice. On a happier note, the special magic of Sachsenring must be those enormous crowds and their behaviour. Opposite the stands at the start/finish line they used to erect tall poles, some of them thirty feet high and supported by rubber guy-lines, and, with a chair and an umbrella, they would sit up there for an incomparable view of the circuit.

EIGHT

The 1980s . . .

Some of the familiar names were still around, but a new decade only served to emphasise, for an old-stager like myself, how different modern motor-cycling was from the days when I raced round Spa, Assen, and the rest. Machines were faster and technically more elaborate and complicated. Riding techniques had changed and it was customary now to move about much more when swinging through corners. The whole racing scene had been sharpened and glamorised, with colourful leathers and space-age helmets. Race contracts were now left much more to the initiative of individual companies in different countries, and sponsorship was big business.

Cecotto was still around. So was Katayama, Walter Villa and a few others, but most of the new lads had strange-sounding names and came from Italy, France, Switzerland, Holland, Germany and, of course, the United States. In 1980 Barry Sheene switched to Yamaha from Suzuki, but his luck changed considerably for the worse. He finished the season in joint fourteenth place with Patrick Pons. Meanwhile, the Kenny Roberts bandwagon rolled on and he secured the 500 cc world championship for the third year running. His main challenge came from fellow-American Randy Mamola, riding a Suzuki machine, who finished the season with 72 points against Roberts's total tally of 87. Marco Lucchinelli, from Italy, riding a Suzuki, was third.

There were new names, too, in the 350 cc class. Jon Ekerold, a talented South African riding a Yamaha, beat the equally talented Anton Mang from West Germany riding a Kawasaki, to take the title by just three points. Kawasaki, through the French rider Jean-François Balde, took third place. Kawasaki dominated the 250 cc class in the way

99

Yamaha had done in the days of Read and Ivy. They occupied the first three positions through Mang, Kork Ballington and Jean-François Balde. Bianchi on the MBA won the 125 cc championship and Lazzarini the 50 cc class on a Kreidler.

One of the big surprises of the season was the performance of Kork Ballington on a Kawasaki in the 500 cc class. Although it was largely unfamiliar territory for both rider and factory, and despite an illness which sidelined him for a spell during the year, Ballington still managed to finish in a creditable twelfth position. Roberts, after three early season victories, was not required to extend himself later, though Randy Mamola's stature grew during the season and he showed that on equal terms he could be a strong and serious challenge to Roberts. Lucchinelli's third position might also well have been an injustice to his talent, for he often raced impressively and was too often afflicted by machine problems.

In 1981 a familiar name was back in the winning lists, Angel Nieto once more taking the 125 cc crown on a Minarelli machine. It was his tenth world title. Tormo, riding a Bultaco, was supreme in 50 cc racing, while the devastating Toni Mang made sure of both the 250 cc and 350 cc titles. In the 500 cc class Marco Lucchinelli turned the tables on Roberts and won the title for Italy for the first time since 1975 and for Suzuki for the first time since 1977. Marco amassed 105 points, Randy Mamola was second with 94 points, and Kenny Roberts dropped to third place with 74 points. Barry Sheene finished in fourth place with 72 points.

It had been a great season and, in the 500 cc class, the hardest-fought for many years, with Yamaha and Suzuki the main protagonists. Kawasaki battled valiantly to make their four-cylinder two strokes more competitive and Ballington did well to finish in eighth position. It was an interesting season too. Roberts's disappointing placing was not a true reflection of his riding talent, for his new Yamaha proved troublesome, while Sheene, whom many were beginning to place on the wrong side of the hill, showed he cannot yet be ignored and may well come back to challenge the world title even more strongly.

At the end of another season, motor-cycle racing was

vibrant and highly competitive, both in rider talent and machinery. And the immediate future looked as good and as bright as at any time in the past. After repeated rumours of a return to racing by Honda, and a disastrous effort with the four-stroke NR in 1980, the news was confirmed: Honda would definitely be back to full-scale grand-prix competition in 1982, with a new two-stroke machine, the first-ever racing two-stroke to come from the famous factory. To prove it all they offered Marco Lucchinelli the biggest contract ever in motor-cycle racing – a two-year term in exchange for £700,000! With that, plus what was said to be a big-money contract for Sheene and lots of talk about turbos, what was the business coming to . . .?

Britain's Lost Riders

British and Commonwealth riders used to dominate the world championships when I was racing in the grands prix. How different it all is today. In the prestigious 500 cc class Barry Sheene was the only British name appearing in the top twenty final placings in 1980. There was Kork Ballington from South Africa and Graeme Crosby from New Zealand. Italy and the United States are now the countries producing most of the top riders.

The rot in Britain started once the Americans focused their sights on Europe. For many years, because of a row between the FIM and the American Motor Cycle Federation, American riders were not permitted to race in Europe. Once the ban was lifted, and Formula 750 cc racing took root, on machines similar to the big Harley-Davidsons on which American racing had been structured, the Americans became interested in racing on the grand-prix circuits in Europe. Britain's regular Transatlantic Road Race Series over the Easter weekend gave them the taste, and there was always the major temptation of winning a world championship.

The first American to win a world-championship grand-prix round was Pat Hennen, who beat a strong challenge from Giacomo Agostini and Tepi Lansivuori to win the 500 cc race

101

of the Finnish Grand Prix in 1976. Steve Baker took the Formula 750 cc world championship in 1976 and in 1978 Kenny Roberts became the first American ever to win the 500 cc world championship in all its 30 years' history. He beat Barry Sheene by just ten points. He won the championship again in 1979 and 1980. His margin of victory in 1979 was by a convincing 24 points over Italy's Virginio Ferrari. In 1980 only 15 points separated him from fellow-American Randy Mamola.

If the Americans retain their interest in the world championships they look certain to make an enormous impact. Riders like Roberts, and the new generation of Randy Mamola and Freddy Spencer (and others who perhaps have yet to make their debut in Europe), are exciting personalities as well as talented and very fast racers. Their presence at a grand prix can send a buzz of anticipation round the track and add thousands to the crowd.

In the late 1970s and early 1980s Italy regained the rider strength it held in the 1950s, with one major difference: in the 1950s riders like Ubbiali, Ruffo, Provini, Lorenzetti and Ambrosini were unbeatable on lightweight machinery. The new breed of Italian racers follow Agostini's example and gain their success in the 500 cc class. The end-of-season tables give an indication of Italy's strides in rider talent in recent years. In 1976 Marco Lucchinelli and Giacomo Agostini were the only Italians in the top twenty placings in the 500 cc world championship. Their number went up to five in 1977, four in 1978, three in 1979, and four again in 1980. In 1981, with a brilliant performance, Marco Lucchinelli took the 500 cc world championship, the first Italian to do so since Agostini in 1975, and only the fourth Italian to take the premier title in its 33-year history. And there were four other Italian riders in the final top twenty listings.

Sadly, there was little to get excited about from a British standpoint. Sheene fared better than in recent years but was our only serious contender, and with so few other British riders gaining any sort of experience of grand-prix racing, the chance of a world championship coming our way in the next few years, except through Barry, seems remote indeed.

The Ill-Fated World Series

I watched with interest the efforts of journalist Barry Coleman and riders Kenny Roberts, Barry Sheene and others to
organise their breakaway World Series in 1980, but I knew
from the start that it was doomed. They went about it the
wrong way. Whatever their personal opinion of the FIM, it
was a plain fact that they needed to carry the official body with
them if the new series was to get off the ground at all. As it
was, they seemed to go out of their way to antagonise it. In the
end the FIM put up the barriers and even though the majority
of the top riders were in favour of the new World Series, it
didn't receive the backing of the factories, and the circuits
dared not support it for fear of reprisals by the FIM, who
control their race licences. It's hardly surprising it never really
got going.

Shrewder tactics and a less pugilistic attitude towards the
FIM might just have pulled it off, for there was a good deal of
support for the World Series. The new arrangement would
have given a better financial deal to the riders and would have
enabled them to ride only on those circuits which they, the
riders, had declared safe. I have enormous sympathy for the
riders, whose battles with the authorities on vital issues like
circuit safety and financial rewards are not confined to the
present generation. I wasn't alone in the 1960s in refusing to
ride on occasion without the promise of start money, and it
was in 1966 that I was involved with riders like John Cooper,
John Hartle, Stuart Graham, Peter Williams, Phil Read, Jim
Redman and others, in forming the Riders Association, an
attempt to foster better relations between organisers and
riders.

The sad thing about the World Series is that its failure will, I
fear, mean that riders will wait a very long time indeed for a
more representative voice in the running of their sport.
Believe me, I am no friend of the FIM, whose high-handed,
dictatorial and often out-of-touch attitude creates many of its
own problems. On the other hand, I can see that running
motor-cycling at an international level, with so many official
world championships, is not as easy a job as Coleman,

Roberts and Co. would seem at times to suggest.

The other problem is that riders themselves hate the idea of being 'organised'. By nature individualistic and used to fighting a lone battle for recognition, they don't take kindly to discipline or compromise in a collective sense. It must also be recognised that the best interests of the crowd-pulling top riders are not always those of the less-well-known riders who make up the entries. So although Kenny Roberts did well in marshalling the top riders, the authorities knew well enough that, when it came to it, there would always be plenty of young hopefuls ready to ride for little more than the chequered flag and a fair chance of glory.

The official announcement of the World Series was made at Silverstone in 1979. The intention was that forty of the world's top riders would boycott the 1980 world-championship events and compete instead in a big-money World Series staged at FIM-sanctioned meetings. Roberts said that the riders were fed up with risking their necks for nothing. Among those who pledged support were Barry Sheene, Virginio Ferrari, Franco Uncini, Wil Hartog, Kork Ballington, Gregg Hansford and Graziano Rossi. The idea was to run 500 cc and 250 cc races, to be known as Formula 1 and Formula 2 on carefully selected circuits with plenty of sponsorship and media interest. A number of non-contracted riders would be invited to race in each event and there would be qualifying heats to select the finalists.

The basic idea behind the World Series was not new. Motor-racing had done it earlier, resulting in the Formula 1 racers running much more of their own show through their representative Bernie Ecclestone, but with the blessing of the FIA, the international governing body of the four-wheel sport. And that's the difference. While Roberts's rebel riders theoretically acknowledged the need to work with the FIM in getting their idea through, in the end, for whatever the reasons, they tried to go it alone . . . and failed.

NINE

All the Champions

The following is a complete record of World Champions, listed in descending order of titles gained.

GIACOMO AGOSTINI (ITALY)
15 World Championships (1966 to 1975)

1966: 500 cc (MV)
1967: 500 cc (MV)
1968: 350 cc (MV) and 500 cc (MV)
1969: 350 cc (MV) and 500 cc (MV)
1970: 350 cc (MV) and 500 cc (MV)
1971: 350 cc (MV) and 500 cc (MV)
1972: 350 cc (MV) and 500 cc (MV)
1973: 350 cc (MV)
1974: 350 cc (Yamaha)
1975: 500 cc (Yamaha)

124 Grand Prix wins

The most successful road racer of all time with more world championships than any other rider. His five 350 cc/500 cc double world championships is also a record.

ANGEL NIETO (SPAIN)
10 World Championships (1969 to 1981)

1969: 50 cc (Derbi)
1970: 50 cc (Derbi)

1971: 125 cc (Derbi)
1972: 50 cc (Derbi) and 125 cc (Derbi)
1975: 50 cc (Van Veen Kreidler)
1976: 50 cc (Bultaco)
1977: 50 cc (Bultaco)
1979: 125 cc (Minarelli)
1981: 125 cc (Minarelli)

70 Grand Prix wins

A rider of outstanding ability on the smaller machines and undoubtedly the most successful Spanish racer of all time. He became the first Spaniard to take a world championship and gave the Spanish Derbi factory their first world championship.

MIKE HAILWOOD (GB)
9 World Championships (1961 to 1967)

1961: 250 cc (Honda)
1962: 500 cc (MV)
1963: 500 cc (MV)
1964: 500 cc (MV)
1965: 500 cc (MV)
1966: 250 cc (Honda) and 350 cc (Honda)
1967: 250 cc (Honda) and 350 cc (Honda)

75 Grand Prix wins

A brilliant and distinguished rider and one of the best-loved characters in the business. In 1963 he broke every lap and race record except one in the entire 500 cc world-championship series. He was also the first rider to win three TT races in a week. Left motor-cycle racing in 1968 following the withdrawal of Honda and went car-racing with outstanding success. Returned to motor-cycle racing on the Isle of Man in 1978, winning the Formula 1 TT (which also carried world championship status), and in 1979 he won the Senior TT on a

Suzuki with new race and lap records. He was awarded the GM and the MBE. After finally retiring from racing, he was killed, along with his young daughter, in a domestic road accident in England in 1981.

CARLO UBBIALI (ITALY)
9 World Championships (1951 to 1960)

1951: 125 cc (Mondial)

1955: 125 cc (MV)

1956: 125 cc (MV) and 250 cc (MV)

1958: 125 cc (MV)

1959: 125 cc (MV) and 250 cc (MV)

1960: 125 cc (MV) and 250 cc (MV)

39 Grand Prix wins

Brilliant rider of lightweight machinery, in which he specialised. Until 1967, his nine world titles was a record in the history of the world championships. In 1956 became only the second rider to achieve a 125 cc/250 cc world-championship double in the same year. Retired at the end of 1960.

PHIL READ (GB)
7 World Championships (1964 to 1974)

1964: 250 cc (Yamaha)

1965: 250 cc (Yamaha)

1968: 125 cc (Yamaha) and 250 cc (Yamaha)

1971: 250 cc (Yamaha)

1973: 500 cc (MV Agusta)

1974: 500 cc (MV Agusta)

50 Grand Prix wins

His first world championship in 1964 was the first world title for Yamaha and the first time the 250 cc world championship had been won on a two-stroke machine. Brought Yamaha their first 125 cc/250 cc world championship double in 1968. He had an uncommonly long career and was noted for his rivalry with Bill Ivy in the 1960s and with Giacomo Agostini in the 1970s.

JOHN SURTEES (GB)
7 World Championships (1956 to 1960)

1956: 500 cc (MV)
1958: 350 cc (MV) and 500 cc (MV)
1959: 350 cc (MV) and 500 cc (MV)
1960: 350 cc (MV) and 500 cc (MV)

38 Grand Prix wins

A rider of outstanding dedication, he was also a talented mechanic, serving his engineering apprenticeship at Vincents. He joined the Norton team in 1955 and MV Agusta in 1956. He was the first rider to gain a 350 cc/500 cc world championship double three times in succession, and the first to win the Senior TT three times running. He won 32 Grand Prix races of the 39 held in the 350 cc and 500 cc classes in 1958, 1959 and 1960. He retired from motor-cycle racing in 1960 and became a success in motor-racing. He is still the only man to win world championships on two wheels and four.

JIM REDMAN (RHODESIA)
6 World Championships (1962 to 1965)

1962: 250 cc (Honda) and 350 cc (Honda)
1963: 250 cc (Honda) and 350 cc (Honda)
1964: 350 cc (Honda)
1965: 350 cc (Honda)

44 Grand Prix wins

A naturalised Rhodesian, though was born in London in 1921. A skilful tactician as well as a brilliant rider. All his major successes were on Honda works bikes. He was team captain during their most outstanding racing days. He retired in 1966, after injuring an arm.

GEOFFREY DUKE (GB)
6 World Championships (1951 to 1955)

1951: 350 cc (Norton) and 500 cc (Norton)

1952: 350 cc (Norton)

1953: 500 cc (Gilera)

1954: 500 cc (Gilera)

1955: 500 cc (Gilera)

32 Grand Prix wins

The first rider to win two world championships in the same year, to be honoured with the award of the OBE, and to win four, and then five, world championships. He was also the first rider to win the 500 cc world championship three times running. An immaculate and stylish rider – and certainly the greatest of his day – he was suspended by the FIM in 1956 for supporting a riders' strike at the Dutch TT on a point of principle. He retired at the end of 1959.

KLAUS ENDERS (WEST GERMANY)
6 World Championships (1967 to 1974)

1967: Sidecar (BMW)

1969: Sidecar (BMW)

1970: Sidecar (BMW)

1972: Sidecar (BMW)

1973: Sidecar (BMW)

1974: Sidecar (BMW)

27 Grand Prix wins

In the great tradition of German sidecar racers on German machinery, he entered his BMW-powered outfit in the world championships for the first time in 1966. Started racing in 1960 and began concentrating in sidecar events in 1964. Still the most successful of all sidecar drivers, he retired in 1976.

KORK BALLINGTON (SOUTH AFRICA)
4 World Championships (1978 to 1979)

1978: 250 cc (Kawasaki) and 350 cc (Kawasaki)
1979: 250 cc (Kawasaki) and 350 cc (Kawasaki)

29 Grand Prix wins

Began his competitive career in his native South Africa in 1967 when only sixteen. Won national championships before travelling to Europe. Brought Kawasaki their first 250 cc and 350 cc world championships.

HUGH ANDERSON (NEW ZEALAND)
4 World Championships (1963 to 1965)

1963: 50 cc (Suzuki) and 125 cc (Suzuki)
1964: 50 cc (Suzuki)
1965: 125 cc (Suzuki)

25 Grand Prix wins

First New Zealander to win a world championship, he had exceptional skill on small-capacity machinery, though he began his European racing career riding large-capacity AJS and Norton machines in the early 1960s. He first rode for Suzuki in 1962, and withdrew from the sport in 1966. His double world championship in 1963 was the first achieved on a Suzuki machine.

WALTER VILLA (ITALY)
4 World Championships (1974 to 1976)

1974: 250 cc (Harley-Davidson)

1975: 250 cc (Harley-Davidson)

1976: 250cc (Harley-Davidson) and 350cc (Harley-Davidson)

23 Grand Prix wins

First rider to win three 250 cc world championships three years running and the only rider to win a world championship on Harley-Davidson.

ERIC OLIVER (GB)
4 World Championships (1949 to 1953)

1949: Sidecar (Norton)

1950: Sidecar (Norton)

1951: Sidecar (Norton)

1953: Sidecar (Norton)

17 Grand Prix wins

First-ever sidecar world champion, in 1949, and his record of four sidecar world championships has only been exceeded by Klaus Enders and equalled by Max Deubel. His four world titles was an exclusive record for eleven years. One of only four British riders to win the sidecar world championship in more than thirty years, Oliver retired from competition in 1955 and died in 1981.

MAX DEUBEL (WEST GERMANY)
4 World Championships (1961 to 1964)

1961: Sidecar (BMW)

1962: Sidecar (BMW)

1963: Sidecar (BMW)

1964: Sidecar (BMW)

12 Grand Prix wins

The only rider to win the sidecar world championship four years running and only the second to gain four titles. Was the first sidecar rider to lap the TT course at more than 90 mph (in 1962). He retired at the end of 1966.

ROLF BILAND (SWITZERLAND)
3 World Championships (1978 to 1981)
1978: Sidecar (Beo-Yamaha and TTM Yamaha)
1979: Sidecar B2A (TTM Yamaha)
1981: Sidecar (LCR)

23 Grand Prix wins

The most controversial sidecar rider of modern times because of his innovative Beo-Imagine outfit, which won races and broke lap records with consummate ease, but discarded many of the traditions associated with sidecar racing.

ANTON MANG (WEST GERMANY)
3 World Championships (1980 and 1981)
1980: 250 cc (Kawasaki)
1981: 250 cc (Kawasaki) and 350 cc (Kawasaki)

23 Grand Prix wins

The technical genius of Sepp Schlogl combined with Mang's ability as a rider to put the 250 cc Kawasaki ahead of the opposition in 1980. The West German's form continued to improve in 1981. His double world championship was Kawasaki's third in four years.

LUIGI TAVERI (SWITZERLAND)
3 World Championships (1962 to 1966)

1962: 125 cc (Honda)

1964: 125 cc (Honda)

1966: 125 cc (Honda)

23 Grand Prix wins

The first Swiss rider to gain a road-racing world championship, he retired at the end of 1966.

PIERPAOLO BIANCHI (ITALY)
3 World Championships (1976 to 1980)

1976: 125 cc (Morbidelli)

1977: 125 cc (Morbidelli)

1980: 125 cc (MBA)

21 Grand Prix wins

After winning two titles on Morbidelli he switched to Minarelli in 1978 in an effort to make it three in a row, but finished third after Lazzarini and Nieto.

EUGENIO LAZZARINI (ITALY)
3 World Championships (1978 to 1980)

1978: 125 cc (MBA)

1979: 50 cc (Van Veen Kreidler)

1980: 50 cc (Van Veen Kreidler)

17 Grand Prix wins

A talented engineer as well as rider, he designed and made the frame of the bike he rode to win his first championship in 1978. Despite tougher opposition, he took his second title the following year.

113

KENNY ROBERTS (USA)
3 World Championships (1978 to 1980)

1978: 500 cc (Yamaha)

1979: 500 cc (Yamaha)

1980: 500 cc (Yamaha)

17 Grand Prix wins

First American to win a road-racing world championship (1978). Most successful American contesting the grands prix in the late 1970s and early 1980s. Was prominent in the unsuccessful challenge to FIM authority in world-championship racing in 1980.

HANS-GEORG ANSCHEIDT (WEST GERMANY)
3 World Championships (1966 to 1968)

1966: 50 cc (Suzuki)

1967: 50 cc (Suzuki)

1968: 50 cc (Suzuki)

14 Grand Prix wins

The first rider in 50 cc competition to win three world championships in three consecutive years. Retired at the end of 1968.

WERNER HAAS (WEST GERMANY)
3 World Championships (1953 and 1954)

1953: 125 cc (NSU) and 250 cc (NSU)

1954: 250 cc (NSU)

11 Grand Prix wins

First German to win a world championship and only the second rider to gain two world titles in the same season. After retiring from racing he was killed in an accident in 1955.

BRUNO RUFFO (ITALY)
3 World Championships (1949 to 1951)

1949: 250 cc (Guzzi)

1950: 125 cc (Mondial)

1951: 250 cc (Guzzi)

4 Grand Prix wins

Equally at ease on 500 cc twin-cylinder machines and light-weights, he was the first rider to win three world titles in three years.

BARRY SHEENE (GB)
2 World Championships (1976 and 1977)

1976: 500 cc (Suzuki)

1977: 500 cc (Suzuki)

19 Grand Prix wins

The most popular British racer of the 1970s and early 1980s with an enormous fan following, winning or not. The first rider to win the 500 cc world championship on a Suzuki machine.

KENT ANDERSSON (SWEDEN)
2 World Championships (1973 and 1974)

1973: 125 cc (Yamaha)

1974: 125 cc (Yamaha)

18 Grand Prix wins

First Swedish rider to capture a motor-cycling world title. Andersson turned to circuit racing after breaking his back in a domestic motor-cycle accident, considering it safer to race on tracks than on public highways. Retired in 1976.

115

GARY HOCKING (RHODESIA)
2 World Championships (1961)

1961: 350 cc (MV) and 500 cc (MV)

18 Grand Prix wins

After becoming world champion in 1961, he retired from racing after his friend Tom Phillis was killed, and returned to Rhodesia. He was tempted to race cars later that year and was killed while practising for the Natal Grand Prix in 1962.

RICARDO TORMO (SPAIN)
2 World Championships (1978 to 1981)

1978: 50 cc (Bultaco)

1981: 50 cc (Bultaco)

17 Grand Prix wins

Initially with Bultaco as second string to Angel Nieto, he got his chance when Nieto began to lose interest in the class.

FRITZ SCHEIDEGGER (SWITZERLAND)
2 World Championships (1965 and 1966)

1965: Sidecar (BMW)

1966: Sidecar (BMW)

16 Grand Prix wins

The first non-German rider to win the sidecar world championship for eleven years. He and passenger John Robinson were going for their third consecutive world title when Scheidegger was killed at a non-grand-prix event at Mallory Park in 1967.

JAN DE VRIES (HOLLAND)
2 World Championships (1971 and 1973)

1971: 50 cc (Kreidler)

1973: 50 cc (Van Veen)

14 Grand Prix wins

Holland's first road-racing world champion, he retired at the end of 1973.

DIETER BRAUN (WEST GERMANY)
2 World Championships (1970 and 1973)

1970: 125 cc (Suzuki)

1973: 250 cc (Yamaha)

13 Grand Prix wins

The West German rider turned to serious racing after competing in motocross events and, briefly, in car racing. A crash in 1973 at the West German Grand Prix shortened his career.

FERGUS ANDERSON (GB)
2 World Championships (1953 and 1954)

1953: 350 cc (Guzzi)

1954: 350 cc (Guzzi)

12 Grand Prix wins

Headed Moto Guzzi's racing department after his retirement from racing at the end of 1954, but later resigned the appointment on a point of principle and was killed in 1956 in a non-world-championship race at Floreffe on a 500 cc BMW. He was also a successful journalist.

117

ROLF STEINHAUSEN (WEST GERMANY)
2 World Championships (1975 and 1976)

1975: Sidecar (Busch Konig)

1976: Sidecar (Busch Konig)

12 Grand Prix wins

He began solo racing at 18, but after crashing at Nurburgring and following a severe skiing accident, he switched to sidecar racing.

HELMUT FATH (WEST GERMANY)
2 World Championships (1960 and 1968)

1960: Sidecar (BMW)

1968: Sidecar (URS)

11 Grand Prix wins

Famous German sidecar racer and the only road-racer to win a world title with a machine powered by an engine designed by himself – the Urs (taken from his hometown of Ursenbach) in 1967, breaking the 14-year monopoly of BMW.

BILL LOMAS (GB)
2 World Championships (1955 and 1956)

1955: 350 cc (Guzzi)

1956: 350 cc (Guzzi)

8 Grand Prix wins

In 1955 brought Moto Guzzi their sixth world championship, a better record than any other factory. A bad fall at Imola in early 1957 led to his retirement.

WILHELM NOLL (WEST GERMANY)
2 World Championships (1954 and 1956)

1954: Sidecar (BMW)

1956: Sidecar (BMW)

8 Grand Prix wins

Responsible for ending the five-year success of Britain in the sidecar class and the start of the 14-year BMW domination. He retired after 1956.

WALTER SCHNEIDER (WEST GERMANY)
2 World Championships (1958 and 1959)

1958: Sidecar (BMW)

1959: Sidecar (BMW)

6 Grand Prix wins

His two world titles were fought against formidable opposition from Florian Camathias. He retired after 1959 to go motor-racing, but the switch was not successful.

UMBERTO MASETTI (ITALY)
2 World Championships (1950 and 1952)

1950: 500 cc (Gilera)

1952: 500 cc (Gilera)

5 Grand Prix wins

A former rider of 125 cc machinery, he beat Geoffrey Duke to the 1950 500 cc title by just one point. After 1952 he rode for MV Agusta. He retired in 1957, and went to live in the Argentine but rode in several grands prix in that country in the 1960s.

119

CECIL SANDFORD (GB)
2 World Championships (1952 to 1957)

1952: 125 cc (MV)

1957: 250 cc (Mondial)

5 Grand Prix wins

First British rider to win the 125 cc world championship and also the 250 cc world championship, and the first rider to win a world championship on an MV Agusta machine. Retired in 1957, while still at the height of his career.

BILL IVY (GB)
1 World Championship (1967)

1967: 125 cc (Yamaha)

21 Grand Prix wins

Rode the first 100 mph lap on a 125 cc machine on the Isle of Man course in 1968, and after his feud with Yamaha team mate Phil Read, left racing, only to be tempted back by the Jawa factory. Was killed on the Jawa in 1969 while practising for the East German Grand Prix at Sachsenring.

TARQUINIO PROVINI (ITALY)
1 World Championship (1958)

1958: 250 cc (MV)

18 Grand Prix wins

His twelve Italian championships was a record for many years. Born in 1930 and retired from racing in 1966.

JOHNNY CECOTTO (VENEZUELA)
1 World Championship (1975)

1975: 350 cc (Yamaha)

14 Grand Prix wins

Real name Alberto, 'Johnny' Cecotto, born in Venezuela, became the youngest rider ever to win a world championship in any category when he secured the 350 cc title in 1975.

ERNST DEGNER (EAST GERMANY)
1 World Championship (1962)

1962: 50 cc (Suzuki)

14 Grand Prix wins

First 50 cc world champion and the first rider to win a world championship on a Suzuki machine. A fine development engineer, his defection from East Germany to the West cost him the world title in 1963. After a fall in the Japanese Grand Prix, he wasn't able to recapture his previous form and he retired in 1965.

JARNO SAARINEN (FINLAND)
1 World Championship (1972)

1972: 250 cc (Yamaha)

13 Grand Prix wins

Competed in ice-racing and speedway before turning to road-racing in 1964. Brilliantly successful in 1972 and 1973. Was leading the 250 cc and 500 cc championship tables in 1973 when he was killed racing at Monza, Italy.

121

RODNEY GOULD (GB)
1 World Championship (1970)

1970: 250 cc (Yamaha)

10 Grand Prix wins

Took his world championship conclusively with six victories and two second places from twelve events. Retired in 1972 to join the Yamaha organisation in Europe, handling racing and public relations.

DAVE SIMMONDS (GB)
1 World Championship (1969)

1969: 125 cc (Kawasaki)

10 Grand Prix wins

First rider to bring Kawasaki a world title. Died in a fire tragedy on the eve of a race in Paris in 1972.

TAKAZUMI KATAYAMA (JAPAN)
1 World Championship (1977)

1977: 350 cc (Yamaha)

9 Grand Prix wins

First Japanese to win a road-racing world championship.

LES GRAHAM (GB)
1 World Championship (1949)

1949: 500 cc (AJS)

8 Grand Prix wins

First 500 cc world champion, in 1949, and in 1950 ended the season in third place in both the 500 cc and 250 cc classes. Crashed fatally in the Senior TT in 1953.

PAOLO PILERI (ITALY)
1 World Championship (1975)

1975: 125 cc (Morbidelli)

8 Grand Prix wins

World-championship winner in his first full season of grand-prix racing.

RALPH BRYANS (IRELAND)
1 World Championship (1965)

1965: 50 cc (Honda)

7 Grand Prix wins

Brought the Honda factory their only 50 cc world championship.

KEL CARRUTHERS (AUSTRALIA)
1 World Championship (1969)

1969: 250 cc (Benelli)

7 Grand Prix wins

First rider to gain positive success and acknowledgement in Australia (his home country), Europe and the United States. Brought Benelli their second world title, in 1969, and their first since Ambrosini's success in 1950. Later left European racing to compete successfully in the American championships. Took over management of Yamaha's international race team on his retirement from racing in 1974.

HENK VAN KESSELL (HOLLAND)
1 World Championship (1974)

1974: 50 cc (Van Veen Kreidler)

7 Grand Prix wins

He began road-racing in 1967 and after making a name for himself in Holland, he took over the machine ridden by Jan de Vries to gain the world championship.

ENRICO LORENZETTI (ITALY)
1 World Championship (1952)

1952: 250 cc (Guzzi)

7 Grand Prix wins

Won his world title at the end of his fifteen years' career in racing by just four points, giving Moto Guzzi their third world championship.

MARCO LUCCHINELLI (ITALY)
1 World Championship (1981)

1981: 500 cc (Suzuki)

6 Grand Prix wins

The easy-going Italian took the 1981 title after a third place in 1980 and finishing 18th in 1979.

TOM PHILLIS (AUSTRALIA)
1 World Championship (1961)

1961: 125 cc (Honda)

6 Grand Prix wins

Honda's first team captain and only the second Australian to win a road-racing world championship. He was killed racing in the 350 cc TT in 1962.

JOCK TAYLOR (GB)
1 World Championship (1981)

1981: Sidecar (Yamaha)

6 Grand Prix wins

Only the fourth British rider to take the sidecar world championship, and the first since O'Dell's victory in 1977.

JON EKEROLD (SOUTH AFRICA)
1 World Championship (1980)

1980: 350 cc (Yamaha)

5 Grand Prix wins

A rider of great determination and courage, he improved from eighth position in 1979 to take the title in 1980 with outstanding lap times. He gained his title on a non-works machine.

FREDDIE FRITH (GB)
1 World Championship (1949)

1949: 350 cc (Velocette)

5 Grand Prix wins

First 350 cc world champion, he rode the first 90 mph lap of the TT course in 1937. Secured his title by winning.all five grands prix in the 350 cc series. Retired from racing after gaining the world title in 1949.

FRITZ HILLEBRAND (WEST GERMANY)
1 World Championship (1957)

1957: Sidecar (BMW)

5 Grand Prix wins

Runner up in 1956, he made certain of the 1957 world title by winning the first three rounds at Hockenheim, on the Isle of Man, and in Holland, but he was killed that year in an international race.

RUPPERT HOLLAUS (AUSTRIA)
1 World Championship (1954)

1954: 125 cc (NSU)

5 Grand Prix wins

First and only Austrian to gain a world title, though his 125 cc world championship was won posthumously. He was killed at the Italian Grand Prix meeting in 1954 after winning all previous rounds.

LIBERO LIBERATI (ITALY)
1 World Championship (1957)

1957: 500 cc (Gilera)

5 Grand Prix wins

His world championship was the last to be won by a Gilera machine and gave the famous Italian factory their sixth world title. He gave up international racing at the end of 1957 on Gilera's withdrawal, but was killed on a touring bike in 1962.

DARIO AMBROSINI (ITALY)
1 World Championship (1950)
1950: 250 cc (Benelli)

4 Grand Prix wins

Was killed at the French Grand Prix at Albi in 1951.

NELLO PAGANI (ITALY)
1 World Championship (1949)
1949: 125 cc (Mondial)

4 Grand Prix wins

The first 125 cc world champion in 1949, he also rode for Gilera and was only one point short of Les Graham's winning total in the 500 cc class that same year.

KEITH CAMPBELL (AUSTRALIA)
1 World Championship (1957)
1957: 250 cc (Guzzi)

3 Grand Prix wins

First Australian to win a road-racing world championship. His success was the last world championship to be gained on a Guzzi machine. After Guzzi's withdrawal from racing at the end of 1957, he continued as a private entrant and was killed while racing at Cadours in 1958.

WILLY FAUST (WEST GERMANY)
1 World Championship (1955)
1955: Sidecar (BMW)

3 Grand Prix wins

His career coincided with the early challenge by BMW to the supremacy in the sidecar class of Norton. His partnership with

Karl Remmert was ended in an accident at Hockenheim in a non-championship outing. Remmert died and Faust suffered severe injuries.

BOB FOSTER (GB)
1 World Championship (1950)

1950: 350 cc (Velocette)

3 Grand Prix wins

Began his racing career in 1934, and was to become a works rider for Moto Guzzi. Retired from racing in 1951.

HORST OWESLE (WEST GERMANY)
1 World Championship (1971)

1971: Sidecar (Urs)

3 Grand Prix wins

After working with famous sidecar champion Helmut Fath, he took over Fath's winning URS machine to gain the world title. He retired at the end of 1971.

CYRIL SMITH (GB)
1 World Championship (1952)

1952: Sidecar (Norton)

2 Grand Prix wins

Second British rider to win a world championship in the sidecar class, and only the third Briton to gain the title in more than thirty years of world-championship sidecar-racing. Retired in 1959 and died in 1962.

BRUNO HOLZER (SWITZERLAND)
1 World Championship (1979)

1979: Sidecar B2B (LCR Yamaha)

1 Grand Prix win

His title was secured by consistent performance. Holzer finished second in all six rounds. He finished sixth in 1980.

MARIO LEGA (ITALY)
1 World Championship (1977)

1977: 250 cc (Morbidelli)

1 Grand Prix win

He got his chance with Morbidelli when Paolo Pileri was injured and showed such promise that the factory loaned him machines.

HERMAN-PETER MULLER (WEST GERMANY)
1 World Championship (1955)

1955: 250 cc (NSU)

1 Grand Prix win

He had been in racing for more than fifteen years when he won his only world championship, after which he retired.

GEORGE O'DELL (GB)
1 World Championship (1977)

1977: Sidecar (Seymaz-Yamaha, Windle-Yamaha)

First British rider to take the title since Eric Oliver's success in 1953. Although he won the title he didn't win one grand prix, but registered the first 100 mph lap of the TT circuit in a sidecar. Died in a domestic incident in 1981 when his body was removed from the burnt-out shell of a house in Hemel Hempstead, Hertfordshire.

TEN

World Championship Results
1949 – 1980 Inclusive

ROAD RACING
World Championships

1949

125 cc
1 Nello Pagani, Italy (Mondial)
2 R. Magi, Italy (Morini)
3 Umberto Masetti, Italy (Morini)

250 cc
1 Bruno Ruffo, Italy (Guzzi)
2 Dario Ambrosini, Italy (Benelli)
3 R. Mead, GB (Mead Norton)

350 cc
1 Freddie Frith, GB (Velocette)
2 Reg Armstrong, Ireland (AJS)
3 Albert Foster, GB (Velocette)

500 cc
1 Les Graham, GB (AJS)
2 Nello Pagani, Italy (Gilera)
3 A. Artesiani, Italy (Gilera)

Sidecar
1 Eric Oliver, GB (Norton)
2 Ercole Frigerio, Italy (Gilera)
3 F. Vanderschrick, Belgium
  (Norton)

1950

125 cc
1 Bruno Ruffo, Italy (Mondial)
2 G. Leoni, Italy (Mondial)
3 Carlo Ubbiali, Italy (Mondial)

250 cc
1 Dario Ambrosini, Italy (Benelli)
2 Maurice Cann, GB (Guzzi)
3 Fergus Anderson, GB (Guzzi)

350 cc
1 Bob Foster, GB (Velocette)
2 Geoffrey Duke, GB (Norton)
3 Les Graham, GB (AJS)

500 cc
1 Umberto Masetti, Italy (Gilera)
2 Geoffrey Duke, GB (Norton)
3 Les Graham, GB (AJS)

Sidecar
1 Eric Oliver, GB (Norton)
2 Ercole Frigerio, Italy (Gilera)
3 Hans Haldemann, Switzerland
  (Norton)

1951

125 cc
1 Carlo Ubbiali, Italy (Mondial)
2 G. Leoni, Italy (Mondial)
3 Bill McCandless, Ireland
  (Mondial)

250 cc
1 Bruno Ruffo, Italy (Guzzi)
2 Tommy Wood, GB (Guzzi)
3 Dario Ambrosini, Italy (Benelli)

350 cc
1 Geoffrey Duke, GB (Norton)
2 Johnny Lockett, GB (Norton)
3 Bill Doran, GB (AJS)

RESULTS TABLE

500 cc
1 Geoffrey Duke, GB (Norton)
2 Alfredo Milani, Italy (Gilera)
3 Umberto Masetti, Italy (Gilera)

Sidecar
1 Eric Oliver, GB (Norton)
2 Ercole Frigerio, Italy (Gilera)
3 Albino Milani, Italy (Gilera)

1952

125 cc
1 Cecil Sandford, GB (MV)
2 Carlo Ubbiali, Italy (Mondial)
3 E. Mendogni, Italy (Morini)

250 cc
1 Enrico Lorenzetti, Italy (Guzzi)
2 Fergus Anderson, GB (Guzzi)
3 Leslie Graham, GB (Velocette)

350 cc
1 Geoffrey Duke, GB (Norton)
2 Reg Armstrong, Ireland (Norton)
3 Ray Amm, Rhodesia (Norton)

500 cc
1 Umberto Masetti, Italy (Gilera)
2 Leslie Graham, GB (MV)
3 Reg Armstrong, Ireland (Norton)

Sidecar
1 Cyril Smith, GB (Norton)
2 Albino Milani, Italy (Gilera)
3 Jacques Drion, France (Norton)

1953

125 cc
1 Werner Haas, W. Germany (NSU)
2 Cecil Sandford, GB (MV)
3 Carlo Ubbiali, Italy (MV)

250 cc
1 Werner Haas, W. Germany (NSU)
2 Reg Armstrong, Ireland (NSU)
3 Fergus Anderson, GB (Guzzi)

350 cc
1 Fergus Anderson, GB (Guzzi)
2 Enrico Lorenzetti, Italy (Guzzi)
3 Ray Amm, Rhodesia (Norton)

500 cc
1 Geoffrey Duke, GB (Gilera)
2 Reg Armstrong, Ireland (Gilera)
3 Alfredo Milani, Italy (Gilera)

Sidecar
1 Eric Oliver, GB (Norton)
2 Cyril Smith, GB (Norton)
3 Hans Haldemann, Switzerland (Norton)

1954

125 cc
1 Ruppert Hollaus, Austria (NSU)
2 Carlo Ubbiali, Italy (MV)
3 Herman Müller, W. Germany (NSU)

250 cc
1 Werner Haas, W. Germany (NSU)
2 Ruppert Hollaus, Austria (NSU)
3 Herman Müller, W. Germany (NSU)

350 cc
1 Fergus Anderson, GB (Guzzi)
2 Ray Amm, Rhodesia (Norton)
3 Rod Coleman, New Zealand (AJS)

500 cc
1 Geoffrey Duke, GB (Gilera)
2 Ray Amm, Rhodesia (Norton)
3 Ken Kavanagh, Australia (Norton)

131

Sidecar
1 Wilhelm Noll, W. Germany (BMW)
2 Eric Oliver, GB (Norton)
3 Cyril Smith, GB (Norton)

1955

125 cc
1 Carlo Ubbiali, Italy (MV)
2 Luigi Taveri, Switzerland (MV)
3 Remo Venturi, Italy (MV)

250 cc
1 Herman Müller, W. Germany (NSU)
2 Cecil Sandford, GB (Guzzi)
3 Bill Lomas, GB (MV)

350 cc
1 Bill Lomas, GB (Guzzi)
2 Dickie Dale, GB (Guzzi)
3 A. Hobl, W. Germany (DKW)

500 cc
1 Geoffrey Duke, GB (Gilera)
2 Reg Armstrong, Ireland (Gilera)
3 Umberto Masetti, Italy (MV)

Sidecar
1 Willy Faust, W. Germany (BMW)
2 Wilhelm Noll, W. Germany (BMW)
3 Walter Schneider, W. Germany (BMW)

1956

125 cc
1 Carlo Ubbiali, Italy (MV)
2 R. Ferri, Italy (Gilera)
3 Luigi Taveri, Switzerland (MV)

250 cc
1 Carlo Ubbiali, Italy (MV)
2 Luigi Taveri, Switzerland (MV)
3 Enrico Lorenzetti, Italy (Guzzi)

350 cc
1 Bill Lomas, GB (Guzzi)
2 A. Hobl, W. Germany (DKW)
3 Dickie Dale, GB (Guzzi)

500 cc
1 John Surtees, GB (MV)
2 Walter Zeller, W. Germany (BMW)
3 John Hartle, GB (Norton)

Sidecar
1 Wilhelm Noll, W. Germany (BMW)
2 Fritz Hillebrand, W. Germany (BMW)
3 Pip Harris, GB (Norton)

1957

125 cc
1 Tarquinio Provini, Italy (Mondial)
2 Luigi Taveri, Switzerland (MV)
3 Carlo Ubbiali, Italy (MV)

250 cc
1 Cecil Sandford, GB (Mondial)
2 Tarquinio Provini, Italy (Mondial)
3 Sammy Miller, Ireland (Mondial)

350 cc
1 Keith Campbell, Australia (Guzzi)
2 Bob McIntyre, Scotland (Gilera)
3 Libero Liberati, Italy (Gilera)

500 cc
1 Libero Liberati, Italy (Gilera)
2 Bob McIntyre, Scotland (Gilera)
3 John Surtees, GB (MV)

Sidecar
1 Fritz Hillebrand, W. Germany (BMW)

2 Walter Schneider, W. Germany
  (BMW)
3 Florian Camathias, Switzerland
  (BMW)

1958

125 cc
1 Carlo Ubbiali, Italy (MV)
2 A. Gandossi, Italy (Ducati)
3 Luigi Taveri, Switzerland
  (Ducati)

250 cc
1 Tarquinio Provini, Italy (MV)
2 H. Fugner, E. Germany (MZ)
3 Carlo Ubbiali, Italy (MV)

350 cc
1 John Surtees, GB (MV)
2 John Hartle, GB (MV)
3 Geoffrey Duke, GB (Norton)

500 cc
1 John Surtees, GB (MV)
2 John Hartle, GB (MV)
3 Dickie Dale, GB (BMW)

Sidecar
1 Walter Schneider, W. Germany
  (BMW)
2 Florian Camathias, Switzerland
  (BMW)
3 Helmut Fath, W. Germany
  (BMW)

1959

125 cc
1 Carlo Ubbiali, Italy (MV)
2 Tarquinio Provini, Italy (MV)
3 Mike Hailwood, GB (Ducati)

250 cc
1 Carlo Ubbiali, Italy (MV)
2 Tarquinio Provini, Italy (MV)
3 Gary Hocking, Rhodesia (MZ)

350 cc
1 John Surtees, GB (MV)
2 John Hartle, GB (MV)
3 Bob Brown, Australia (Norton)

500 cc
1 John Surtees, GB (MV)
2 Remo Venturi, Italy (MV)
3 Bob Brown, Australia (Norton)

Sidecar
1 Walter Schneider, W. Germany
  (BMW)
2 Florian Camathias, Switzerland
  (BMW)
3 Fritz Scheidegger, Switzerland
  (BMW)

1960

125 cc
1 Carlo Ubbiali, Italy (MV)
2 Gary Hocking, Rhodesia (MV)
3 Ernst Degner, E. Germany
  (MZ)

250 cc
1 Carlo Ubbiali, Italy (MV)
2 Gary Hocking, Rhodesia (MV)
3 Luigi Taveri, Switzerland (MV)

350 cc
1 John Surtees, GB (MV)
2 Gary Hocking, Rhodesia (MV)
3 John Hartle, GB (MV/Norton)

500 cc
1 John Surtees, GB (MV)
2 Remo Venturi, Italy (MV)
3 John Hartle, GB (Norton/MV)

Sidecar
1 Helmut Fath, W. Germany
  (BMW)
2 Fritz Scheidegger, Switzerland
  (BMW)
3 Pip Harris, GB (BMW)

133

1961

125 cc
1 Tom Phillis, Australia (Honda)
2 Ernst Degner, E. Germany (MZ)
3 Luigi Taveri, Switzerland (Honda)

250 cc
1 Mike Hailwood, GB (Honda)
2 Tom Phillis, Australia (Honda)
3 Jim Redman, Rhodesia (Honda)

350 cc
1 Gary Hocking, Rhodesia (MV)
2 Frantisek Stastny, Czechoslovakia (Jawa)
3 G. Havel, Czechoslovakia (Jawa)

500 cc
1 Gary Hocking, Rhodesia (MV)
2 Mike Hailwood, GB (Norton/MV)
3 Frank Perris, GB (Norton)

Sidecar
1 Max Deubel, W. Germany (BMW)
2 Fritz Scheidegger, Switzerland (BMW)
3 E. Strub, Switzerland (BMW)

1962

50 cc
1 Ernst Degner, W. Germany (Suzuki)
2 Hans-Georg Anscheidt, W. Germany (Kreidler)
3 Luigi Taveri, Switzerland (Honda)

125 cc
1 Luigi Taveri, Switzerland (Honda)
2 Jim Redman, Rhodesia (Honda)
3 Tommy Robb, Ireland (Honda)

250 cc
1 Jim Redman, Rhodesia (Honda)
2 Bob McIntyre, Scotland (Honda)
3 A. Wheeler, GB (Guzzi)

350 cc
1 Jim Redman, Rhodesia (Honda)
2 Mike Hailwood, GB (MV)
3 Tommy Robb, Ireland (Honda)

500 cc
1 Mike Hailwood, GB (MV)
2 Alan Shepherd, GB (Matchless)
3 Phil Read, GB (Norton)

Sidecar
1 Max Deubel, W. Germany (BMW)
2 Florian Camathias, Switzerland (BMW)
3 Fritz Scheidegger, Switzerland (BMW)

1963

50 cc
1 Hugh Anderson, New Zealand (Suzuki)
2 Hans-Georg Anscheidt, W. Germany (Kreidler)
3 Ernst Degner, W. Germany (Suzuki)

125 cc
1 Hugh Anderson, New Zealand (Suzuki)
2 Luigi Taveri, Switzerland (Honda)
3 Jim Redman, Rhodesia (Honda)

250 cc
1 Jim Redman, Rhodesia (Honda)
2 Tarquinio Provini, Italy (Morini)
3 Fumio Ito, Japan (Yamaha)

134

350 cc
1 Jim Redman, Rhodesia (Honda)
2 Mike Hailwood, GB (MV)
3 Luigi Taveri, Switzerland
  (Honda)

500 cc
1 Mike Hailwood, GB (MV)
2 Alan Shepherd, GB (Matchless)
3 John Hartle, GB (Gilera)

Sidecar
1 Max Deubel, W. Germany
  (BMW)
2 Florian Camathias, Switzerland
  (BMW)
3 Fritz Scheidegger, Switzerland
  (BMW)

1964

50 cc
1 Hugh Anderson, New Zealand
  (Suzuki)
2 Ralph Bryans, Ireland (Honda)
3 Hans-Georg Anscheidt, W.
  Germany (Kreidler)

125 cc
1 Luigi Taveri, Switzerland
  (Honda)
2 Jim Redman, Rhodesia (Honda)
3 Hugh Anderson, New Zealand
  (Suzuki)

250 cc
1 Phil Read, GB (Yamaha)
2 Jim Redman, Rhodesia (Honda)
3 Alan Shepherd, GB (MZ)

350 cc
1 Jim Redman, Rhodesia (Honda)
2 Bruce Beale, Rhodesia (Honda)
3 Mike Duff, Canada (AJS)

500 cc
1 Mike Hailwood, GB (MV)

2 Jack Ahearn, Australia (Norton)
3 Phil Read, GB (Matchless)

Sidecar
1 Max Deubel, W. Germany
  (BMW)
2 Fritz Scheidegger, Switzerland
  (BMW)
3 Colin Seeley, GB (BMW)

1965

50 cc
1 Ralph Bryans, Ireland (Honda)
2 Luigi Taveri, Switzerland
  (Honda)
3 Hugh Anderson, New Zealand
  (Suzuki)

125 cc
1 Hugh Anderson, New Zealand
  (Suzuki)
2 Frank Perris, GB (Suzuki)
3 Denis Woodman, GB (MZ)

250 cc
1 Phil Read, GB (Yamaha)
2 Mike Duff, Canada (Yamaha)
3 Jim Redman, Rhodesia (Honda)

350 cc
1 Jim Redman, Rhodesia (Honda)
2 Giacomo Agostini, Italy (MV)
3 Mike Hailwood, GB (MV)

500 cc
1 Mike Hailwood, GB (MV)
2 Giacomo Agostini, Italy (MV)
3 Paddy Driver, S. Africa
  (Matchless)

Sidecar
1 Fritz Scheidegger, Switzerland
  (BMW)
2 Max Deubel, W. Germany
  (BMW)

3 Georg Auerbacher, W.
Germany (BMW)

1966

50 cc

1 Hans-Georg Anscheidt, W.
Germany (Suzuki)
2 Ralph Bryans, Ireland (Honda)
3 Luigi Taveri, Switzerland
(Honda)

125 cc

1 Luigi Taveri, Switzerland
(Honda)
2 Bill Ivy, GB (Yamaha)
3 Ralph Bryans, Ireland (Honda)

250 cc

1 Mike Hailwood, GB (Honda)
2 Phil Read, GB (Yamaha)
3 Jim Redman, Rhodesia (Honda)

350 cc

1 Mike Hailwood, GB (Honda)
2 Giacomo Agostini, Italy (MV)
3 Renzo Pasolini, Italy
(Aermacchi)

500 cc

1 Giacomo Agostini, Italy (MV)
2 Mike Hailwood, GB (Honda)
3 Jack Findlay, Australia
(Matchless)

Sidecar

1 Fritz Scheidegger, Switzerland
(BMW)
2 Max Deubel, W. Germany
(BMW)
3 Colin Seeley, GB (BMW)

1967

50 cc

1 Hans-Georg Anscheidt, W.
Germany (Suzuki)

2 Yoshi Katayama, Japan (Suzuki)
3 Stuart Graham, GB (Suzuki)

125 cc

1 Bill Ivy, GB (Yamaha)
2 Phil Read, GB (Yamaha)
3 Stuart Graham, GB (Suzuki)

250 cc

1 Mike Hailwood, GB (Honda)
2 Phil Read, GB (Yamaha)
3 Bill Ivy, GB (Yamaha)

350 cc

1 Mike Hailwood, GB (Honda)
2 Giacomo Agostini, Italy (MV)
3 Ralph Bryans, Ireland (Honda)

500 cc

1 Giacomo Agostini, Italy (MV)
2 Mike Hailwood, GB (Honda)
3 John Hartle, GB (Matchless)

Sidecar

1 Klaus Enders, W. Germany
(BMW)
2 Georg Auerbacher, W.
Germany (BMW)
3 Siegfried Schauzu, W. Germany
(BMW)

1968

50 cc

1 Hans-Georg Anscheidt, W.
Germany (Suzuki)
2 P. Lodewijkx, Holland
(Jamathi)
3 B. Smith, Australia (Derbi)

125 cc

1 Phil Read, GB (Yamaha)
2 Bill Ivy, GB (Yamaha)
3 Ginger Molloy, New Zealand
(Bultaco)

136

250 cc
1 Phil Read, GB (Yamaha)
2 Bill Ivy, GB (Yamaha)
3 Heinz Rosner, E. Germany
  (MZ)

350 cc
1 Giacomo Agostini, Italy (MV)
2 Renzo Pasolini, Italy (Benelli)
3 Kel Carruthers, Australia
  (Aermacchi)

500 cc
1 Giacomo Agostini, Italy (MV)
2 Jack Findlay, Australia
  (Matchless)
3 Gyula Marsovszky, Switzerland
  (Matchless)

Sidecar
1 Helmut Fath, W. Germany
  (URS)
2 Georg Auerbacher, W.
  Germany (BMW)
3 Siegfried Schauzu, W. Germany
  (BMW)

1969

50 cc
1 Angel Nieto, Spain (Derbi)
2 Aalt Toersen, Holland
  (Kreidler)
3 B. Smith, Australia (Derbi)

125 cc
1 Dave Simmonds, GB
  (Kawasaki)
2 Dieter Braun, W. Germany
  (Suzuki)
3 C. van Dongen, Holland
  (Suzuki)

250 cc
1 Kel Carruthers, Australia
  (Benelli)

2 Kent Andersson, Sweden
  (Yamaha)
3 Santiago Herrero, Spain (Ossa)

350 cc
1 Giacomo Agostini, Italy (MV)
2 Silvio Grassetti, Italy
  (Yamaha/Jawa)
3 G. Visenzi, Italy (Yamaha)

500 cc
1 Giacomo Agostini, Italy (MV)
2 Gyula Marsovszky, Switzerland
  (Linto)
3 G. Nash, GB (Norton)

Sidecar
1 Klaus Enders, W. Germany
  (BMW)
2 Helmut Fath, W. Germany
  (URS)
3 Georg Auerbacher, W.
  Germany (BMW)

1970

50 cc
1 Angel Nieto, Spain (Derbi)
2 Aalt Toersen, Holland (Jamathi)
3 Rudolph Kunz, W. Germany
  (Kreidler)

125 cc
1 Dieter Braun, W. Germany
  (Suzuki)
2 Angel Nieto, Spain (Derbi)
3 Borje Jansson, Sweden
  (Maico)

250 cc
1 Rodney Gould, GB (Yamaha)
2 Kel Carruthers, Australia
  (Yamaha)
3 Kent Andersson, Sweden
  (Yamaha)

137

350 cc
1 Giacomo Agostini, Italy (MV)
2 Kel Carruthers, Australia
  (Benelli/Yamaha)
3 Renzo Pasolini, Italy (Benelli)

500 cc
1 Giacomo Agostini, Italy (MV)
2 Ginger Molloy, New Zealand
  (Kawasaki)
3 Angelo Bergamonti, Italy
  (Aermacchi/MV)

Sidecar
1 Klaus Enders, W. Germany
  (BMW)
2 Georg Auerbacher, W.
  Germany (BMW)
3 Siegfreid Schauzu, W. Germany
  (BMW)

1971

50 cc
1 Jan de Vries, Holland (Kreidler)
2 Angel Nieto, Spain (Derbi)
3 J. Schurgers, Holland (Kreidler)

125 cc
1 Angel Nieto, Spain (Derbi)
2 Barry Sheene, GB (Suzuki)
3 Borje Jansson, Sweden (Maico)

250 cc
1 Phil Read, GB (Yamaha)
2 Rodney Gould, GB (Yamaha)
3 Jarno Saarinen, Finland
  (Yamaha)

350 cc
1 Giacomo Agostini, Italy (MV)
2 Jarno Saarinen, Finland
  (Yamaha)
3 K-I. Carlsson, Sweden
  (Yamaha)

500 cc
1 Giacomo Agostini, Italy (MV)
2 K. Turner, New Zealand
  (Suzuki)
3 R. Bron, Holland (Suzuki)

Sidecar
1 Horst Owesle, W. Germany
  (Munch)
2 A. Butscher, W. Germany
  (BMW)
3 Siegfreid Schauzu, W. Germany
  (BMW)

1972

50 cc
1 Angel Nieto, Spain (Derbi)
2 Jan de Vries, Holland (Kreidler)
3 Theo Timmer, Holland
  (Jamathi)

125 cc
1 Angel Nieto, Spain (Derbi)
2 Kent Andersson, Sweden
  (Yamaha)
3 Charles Mortimer, GB
  (Yamaha)

250 cc
1 Jarno Saarinen, Finland
  (Yamaha)
2 Renzo Pasolini, Italy
  (Aermacchi)
3 Rodney Gould, GB (Yamaha)

350 cc
1 Giacomo Agostini, Italy (MV)
2 Jarno Saarinen, Finland
  (Yamaha)
3 Renzo Pasolini, Italy
  (Aermacchi)

500 cc
1 Giacomo Agostini, Italy (MV)
2 Alberto Pagani, Italy (MV)
3 Bruno Kneubuhler,
  Czechoslovakia (Yamaha)

RESULTS TABLE

Sidecar
1 Klaus Enders, W. Germany (BMW)
2 Heinz Luthringshauser, W. Germany (BMW)
3 Siegfreid Schauzu, W. Germany (BMW)

Sidecar
1 Klaus Enders, W. Germany (BMW)
2 Werner Schwarzel, W. Germany (Konig)
3 Siegfreid Schauzu, W. Germany (BMW)

1973

50 cc
1 Jan de Vries, Holland (Van Veen Kreidler)
2 Bruno Kneubuhler, Czechoslovakia (Van Veen Kreidler)
3 Theo Timmer, Holland (Jamathi)

125 cc
1 Kent Andersson, Sweden (Yamaha)
2 Charles Mortimer, GB (Yamaha)
3 J. Schurgers, Holland (Bridgestone)

250 cc
1 Dieter Braun, W. Germany (Yamaha)
2 Tepi Lansivuori, Finland (Yamaha)
3 John Dodds, Australia (Yamaha)

350 cc
1 Giacomo Agostini, Italy (MV)
2 Tepi Lansivuori, Finland (Yamaha)
3 Phil Read, GB (MV)

500 cc
1 Phil Read, GB (MV)
2 K. Newcombe, New Zealand (Konig)
3 Giacomo Agostini, Italy (MV)

1974

50 cc
1 Henk van Kessell, Holland (Van Veen Kreidler)
2 Herbert Rittberger, W. Germany (Kreidler)
3 Julien van Zeebroeck, Belgium (Kreidler)

125 cc
1 Kent Andersson, Sweden (Yamaha)
2 Bruno Kneubuhler, Czechoslovakia (Yamaha)
3 Otello Buscherini, Italy (Malanca)
3) Angel Nieto, Spain (Derbi)

250 cc
1 Walter Villa, Italy (Harley-Davidson)
2 Dieter Braun, W. Germany (Yamaha)
3 Patrick Pons, France (Yamaha)

350 cc
1 Giacomo Agostini, Italy (Yamaha)
2 Dieter Braun, W. Germany (Yamaha)
3 Patrick Pons, France (Yamaha)

500 cc
1 Phil Read, GB (MV)
2 Gianfranco Bonera, Italy (MV)
3 Tepi Lansivuori, Finland (Yamaha)

139

Sidecar
1 Klaus Enders, W. Germany
  (Busch BMW)
2 Werner Schwarzel, W. Germany
  (Konig)
3 Siegfreid Schauzu, W. Germany
  (BMW)

Sidecar
1 Rolf Steinhausen, W. Germany
  (Konig)
2 Werner Schwarzel, W. Germany
  (Konig)
3 Rolf Biland, Switzerland
  (Yamaha)

1975

50 cc
1 Angel Nieto, Spain (Kreidler)
2 Eugenio Lazzarine, Italy
  (Piovaticci)
3 Julien van Zeebroeck, Belgium
  (Kreidler)

1976

50 cc
1 Angel Nieto, Spain (Bultaco)
2 Herbert Rittberger, W.
  Germany (Kreidler)
3 Ulrich Graf, Switzerland
  (Kreidler)

125 cc
1 Paolo Pileri, Italy (Morbidelli)
2 Pierpaolo Bianchi, Italy
  (Morbidelli)
3 Kent Andersson, Sweden
  (Yamaha)

125 cc
1 Pierpaolo Bianchi, Italy
  (Morbidelli)
2 Angel Nieto, Spain (Bultaco)
3 Paolo Pileri, Italy
  (Morbidelli)

250 cc
1 Walter Villa, Italy
  (Harley-Davidson)
2 Michel Rougerie, France
  (Harley-Davidson)
3 Dieter Braun, W. Germany
  (Yamaha)

250 cc
1 Walter Villa, Italy
  (Harley-Davidson)
2 Takazumi Katayama, Japan
  (Yamaha)
3 Gianfranco Bonera, Italy
  (Harley-Davidson)

350 cc
1 Johnny Cecotto, Venezuela
  (Yamaha)
2 Giacomo Agostini, Italy
  (Yamaha)
3 Penti Korhonen, Finland
  (Yamaha)

350 cc
1 Walter Villa, Italy
  (Harley-Davidson)
2 Johnny Cecotto, Venezuela
  (Yamaha)
3 Charles Mortimer, GB
  (Yamaha)

500 cc
1 Giacomo Agostini, Italy
  (Yamaha)
2 Phil Read, GB (MV)
3 Hideo Kanaya, Japan (Yamaha)

500 cc
1 Barry Sheene, GB (Suzuki)
2 Tepi Lansivuori, Finland
  (Suzuki)
3 Pat Hennen, USA (Suzuki)

RESULTS TABLE

Sidecar
1 Rolf Steinhausen, W. Germany
  (Busch Konig)
2 Werner Schwarzel, W. Germany
  (Konig)
3 Herman Schmid, Switzerland
  (Yamaha)

1977

50 cc
1 Angel Nieto, Spain (Bultaco)
2 Eugenio Lazzarini, Italy
  (Kreidler)
3 Ricardo Tormo, Spain (Bultaco)

125 cc
1 Pierpaolo Bianchi, Italy
  (Morbidelli)
2 Eugenio Lazzarini, Italy
  (Morbidelli)
3 Angel Nieto, Spain (Bultaco)

250 cc
1 Mario Lega, Italy (Morbidelli)
2 Franco Uncini, Italy
  (Harley-Davidson)
3 Walter Villa, Italy
  (Harley-Davidson)

350 cc
1 Takazumi Katayama, Japan
  (Yamaha)
2 Tom Herron, GB (Yamaha)
3 Jon Ekerold, South Africa
  (Yamaha)

500 cc
1 Barry Sheene, GB (Suzuki)
2 Steve Baker, USA (Yamaha)
3 Pat Hennen, USA (Suzuki)

Sidecar
1 George O'Dell, GB
  (Seymaz-Yamaha &
  Windle-Yamaha)

2 Rolf Biland, Switzerland
  (Schmid-Yamaha)
3 Werner Schwarzel, W. Germany
  (Aro)

Formula 750
1 Steve Baker, USA (Yamaha)
2 Christian Sarron, France
  (Yamaha)
3 Giacomo Agostini, Italy
  (Yamaha)

1978

50 cc
1 Ricardo Tormo, Spain (Bultaco)
2 Eugenio Lazzarini, Italy
  (Kreidler)
3 Patrick Plisson, France (ABF)

125 cc
1 Eugenio Lazzarini, Italy (MBA)
2 Angel Nieto, Spain
  (Bultaco/Minarelli)
3 Pierpaolo Bianchi, Italy
  (Minarelli)

250 cc
1 Kork Ballington, S. Africa
  (Kawasaki)
2 Gregg Hansford, Australia
  (Kawasaki)
3 Patrick Fernandez, France
  (Yamaha)

350 cc
1 Kork Ballington, S. Africa
  (Kawasaki)
2 Takazumi Katayama, Japan
  (Yamaha)
3 Gregg Hansford, Australia
  (Kawasaki)

500 cc
1 Kenny Roberts, USA (Yamaha)
2 Barry Sheene, GB (Suzuki)
3 Johnny Cecotto, Venezuela
  (Yamaha)

Sidecar
1 Rolf Biland, Switzerland
(Beo-Yamaha & TTM
Yamaha)
2 Alain Michel, France
(Seymaz-Yamaha)
3 Bruno Holzer, Switzerland
(LCR-Yamaha)

Formula 750
1 Johnny Cecotto, Venezuela
(Yamaha)
2 Kenny Roberts, USA (Yamaha)
3 Christian Sarron, France
(Yamaha)

1979

50 cc
1 Eugenio Lazzarini, Italy
(Kreidler)
2 Rolf Blatter, Switzerland
(Kreidler)
3 Patrick Plisson, France (ABF)

125 cc
1 Angel Nieto, Spain (Minarelli)
2 Maurizio Massimiani, Italy
(Morbidelli)
3 Hans Müller, Switzerland
(MBA)

250 cc
1 Kork Ballington, S. Africa
(Kawasaki)
2 Gregg Hansford, Australia
(Kawasaki)
3 Graziano Rossi, Italy
(Morbidelli)

350 cc
1 Kork Ballington, S. Africa
(Kawasaki)
2 Patrick Fernandez, France
(Yamaha)
3 Gregg Hansford, Australia
(Kawasaki)

500 cc
1 Kenny Roberts, USA (Yamaha)
2 Virginio Ferrari, Italy (Suzuki)
3 Barry Sheene, GB (Suzuki)

Sidecar B2A
1 Rolf Biland, Switzerland
(Yamaha)
2) Rolf Steinhausen, W. Germany
(Yamaha)
2) Dick Greasley, GB (Yamaha)

Sidecar B2B
1 Bruno Holzer, Switzerland
(LCR)
2 Rolf Biland, Switzerland (LCR)
3 Masato Kumano, Japan
(Yamaha)

Formula 750
1 Patrick Pons, France (Yamaha)
2 Michel Frutschi, Switzerland
(Yamaha)
3 Johnny Cecotto, Venezuela
(Yamaha)

1980

50 cc
1 Eugenio Lazzarini, Italy
(Kreidler/Iprem)
2 Stefan Dorflinger,
Switzerland (Kreidler)
3 Hans Hummel, Austria
(Kreidler)

125 cc
1 Pierpaolo Bianchi, Italy (MBA)
2 Guy Bertin, France
(Motobecane)
3 Angel Nieto, Spain (Minarelli)

250 cc
1 Anton Mang, Germany
(Kawasaki)
2 Kork Ballington, S. Africa
(Kawasaki)

142

3 Jean François Balde, France
(Kawasaki)

350 cc
1 Jon Ekerold, S. Africa
(Yamaha)
2 Anton Mang, Germany
(Kawasaki)
3 Jean-François Balde, France
(Kawasaki)

500 cc
1 Kenny Roberts, USA (Yamaha)
2 Randy Mamola, USA (Suzuki)
3 Marco Lucchinelli, Italy
(Suzuki)

Sidecar
1 Jock Taylor, GB (Yamaha)
· Benga Johansson, Sweden.
2 Rolf Biland, Czechoslovakia
(Yamaha)
Kurt Waltisperg, Czechoslovakia
2 Alain Michel, France (Yamaha)
Paul Gerard, France
Michael Burkhard, Germany

1981

50 cc
1 Ricardo Tormo, Spain (Bultaco)

2 Theo Timmer, Holland
(Bultaco)
3 Stefan Dörflinger, Switzerland
(Kreidler)

125 cc
1 Angel Nieto, Spain (Minarelli)
2 Loris Reggiani, Italy (Minarelli)
3 Pierpaolo Bianchi, Italy (MBA)

250 cc
1 Anton Mang, Germany
(Kawasaki)
2 Jean-François Balde, France
(Kawasaki)
3 Roland Freymond, Switzerland
(Ad Majora)

350 cc
1 Anton Mang, Germany
(Kawasaki)
2 Jon Ekerold, South Africa
(Yamaha)
3 Jean-François Balde, France
(Kawasaki)

500 cc
1 Marco Lucchinelli, Italy (Suzuki)
2 Randy Mamola, USA (Suzuki)
3 Kenny Roberts, USA (Yamaha)

Index

145

INDEX

147

INDEX

Yamaha, 36, 47, 48, 50, 52–8 passim,
70–85 passim, 87, 88, 89, 90, 92, 93,
95, 99, 100, 107–8, 120, 121, 122,
123

Zeebroeck, Julien van, 82
Zeller, Walter, 16
Zolder, 89
Zschopau, 72